W9-BBF-655

U. S. National Bibliography and the Copyright Law

An Historical Study

U. S. National Bibliography and the Copyright Law

AN HISTORICAL STUDY

by Joseph W. Rogers

Foreword by Verner W. Clapp

R. R. BOWKER COMPANY
NEW YORK · 1960

62 West 45th Street, New York 36, N.Y.

Price: $5.00

Library of Congress Catalog Card No. 60-15545

Printed and bound in the United States of America

Foreword

I am delighted to find the Bowker imprint on the title page of this volume in which Joseph Rogers explores the effect of the century-and-a-half quest for an American national bibliography upon the development of copyright legislation in the United States. For in this book we are forcibly reminded of the special place which Richard Rogers Bowker occupies both in the development of bibliographical services in this country and in the architecture of our copyright system. The fact is that the peculiarities of that system derive from and reflect to a not inconsiderable degree the ambition and the effort to achieve a record of the national literary production: the very setting of the Copyright Office within the national library is testimony of this, as are many of the formalities peculiar to our law with which the Copyright Act attempts to assure the completeness and availability of the record. The story of the *Catalog of Copyright Entries,* as unfolded by Mr. Rogers, shows at important points the influence of a man who was not only one of the founders of the American Library Association and the editor of its first official organ, not only the friend and close collaborator of Ainsworth Rand Spofford, Thorvald Solberg, and Herbert Putnam (Dr. Putnam felicitously called him the "incessant observer" for fifty years of the aims, development, and activities of libraries; and Bowker before his death endowed a fund for "bibliographic service" in the national library), but who also represented the book-publishing world as the editor and publisher of its principal trade journal.

Mr. Rogers' assignment did not require him to do so, but he could easily have continued the story. The union of the *Library Journal* and of *Publishers' Weekly,* effected by Richard Rogers Bowker, has continued to this day. The communal property of this alliance is a concern for the publishing and use of books;

and in this common interest they have been potent forces for the development of bibliographic services and for improvements in the copyright system. Certain it is that the present chairman of the board of the company which publishes them both, Frederic G. Melcher, has throughout a long career of multitudinous services to authorship and readership, to publishing and libraries, maintained this duality of interest established by his predecessor.

The interests of the various groups concerned with books —authors, publishers, printers, booksellers, librarians, and the reading public—fortunately tend to parallel each other. Occasionally, however, they seem to diverge, and especially is this so when copyright legislation is pending. Mr. Melcher's capacity for understanding and harmonizing opposing viewpoints has on these occasions served the book world well. In the several attempts in the twenties and thirties to enact legislation to enable the United States to enter the Berne Copyright Union, Mr. Melcher worked tirelessly toward the reconciliation of opposing views in the hope of obtaining partnership for the United States in an international copyright system. And when in 1955 legislation made possible United States ratification of the Universal Copyright Convention, he was one of the important members of the national committee that spearheaded the movement.

And so with the bibliographical record. Mr. Rogers points out the close connection between the bibliographical activities of the Bowker Company and the search of the American library world for a central source of cataloging information which would render unnecessary the repetitive cataloging of the same book in many thousands of separate libraries. His story does not require him to mention that at one point an attempt was made to adapt the entries in Bowker's *American Catalogue* to this purpose, nor that, when Dr. Putnam commenced the distribution of Library of Congress catalog cards in 1901, Mr. Bowker sought to insure the program both with financial aid and with the proffer of office facilities in New York. In more recent years we have seen the service anticipated by Mr. Solberg in his initial bibliographical endeavor—the compilation of an index to the *Publishers' Trade List Annual*—reach fulfillment in the published indexes compiled by A. H. Leypoldt in 1902-04 and currently in *Books in Print* and other important guides to publications issued by Mr. Bowker's successors. And just as the Copyright Act with its provisions for the *Catalog of Copyright Entries* comes once more under scrutiny, we have witnessed the establishment by the Bowker Company of the monthly *American Book Production Record,* a classified recapitulation of the entries from the traditional Weekly Record but now newly reflecting the cataloging information provided by the Library of Congress, and representing a still further advance in the coordination of the procedures for the creation and publication of the record of an important segment of the national bibliography.

The interesting and useful record assembled by Mr. Rogers and presented here in full outline for the first time tells us emphatically that the need for prompt and useful bibliographic information regarding the national book production has increased progressively over the years, and has required to be met from time to time by constantly improved services involving the cooperation of many groups, both private and governmental. It is not likely that this need will be fully met for long by any service now available. Mr. Rogers' work may well contribute to a study of next steps, for which it is not too early to be planning.

VERNER W. CLAPP
President, Council on Library Resources, Inc.
Washington, D.C.

May 3, 1960

Preface

The historical review contained in these pages embodies some of the results of an investigation performed as one phase of the special research program of the Copyright Office, which was authorized by Congress to provide background for the preparation of a general revision of the United States copyright law. The objective of that investigation was to isolate the problems presented by the so-called "cataloging provisions" of the present law (sections 210 and 211 of Title 17, U.S.C.) so that sound decisions could be reached about including such provisions in a new law. The results have been incorporated, through the joint attention of the writer and Mrs. Elizabeth K. Dunne, Copyright Office research analyst, in the *Catalog of Copyright Entries,* one of the series of studies pertaining to copyright law revision produced under this program.

Because the historical background of this problem involves so largely the growth of activities in the United States designed to achieve reliable records of our national intellectual product, it has been considered desirable to make the history of this background available to a wider audience as one aspect, heretofore unreported, of the full story of bibliographical activity in the United States.

I am happy to acknowledge with appreciation the interest and encouragement of the Register of Copyrights, Arthur Fisher, and of the Chairman of the Board of the R. R. Bowker Company, Frederic G. Melcher, in making it possible to issue this historical survey in this form. The Bowker Company has kindly permitted extensive quotation from its publications.

JOSEPH W. ROGERS

Contents

1 Introduction

The cataloging provisions of the present United States copyright law (sections 210 and 211) exist today substantially as they were written prior to the enactment of the law of March 4, 1909. They deal almost exclusively with the publication and distribution of a series of catalogs now called the *Catalog of Copyright Entries.*

The *Catalog of Copyright Entries* (*Catalogue of Title-Entries* prior to July 1906) is a currently compiled serial publication which has been issued without interruption from July 1, 1891, to the present. It lists all the works in which copyright has been claimed and completed by the deposit of copies, and for which certificates of registration have been issued (on request prior to 1909, automatically thereafter), including the essential facts of copyright registration. It also includes renewals of copyright claims registered since 1909. Appropriate indexes of varying kinds have been provided during its existence. In its sixty-seven years of continuous publication (fifty-two of them by the Library of Congress, making it now the Library's oldest regularly issued serial publication other than the Librarian's *Annual Report*) it has listed more than nine million works, comprising the bulk of the United States commercial production of books, periodicals, music, maps, and motion pictures, and large numbers of art works in wide variety. Roughly $2,000,000 have been spent from appropriated funds during this period for printing and binding the *Catalog.*

In addition to the current catalogs, "cumulative," "retrospective," or "consolidated" catalogs have been issued covering dramas for the years 1870-1916 and motion pictures from the beginning of the industry through 1949.

The *Catalog* is the published form of the card record of original and renewal registrations, now maintained as the Copyright Card Catalog. Experience has shown the latter to have a high degree of reliability; it constitutes the principal search tool of the Copyright Office Reference Search Section and for most inquiries serves in place of the applications for copyright registration, although it is auxiliary both to the applications and to available deposit copies. The applications, submitted by claimants and containing information required for registration, are arranged and maintained in registration number order—in effect, chronologically by date of registration. The card catalog, in contrast, is arranged alphabetically by commonly used descriptive elements, usually title, author, and copyright proprietor. Duplicates of the card entries in some classes are secured by performing-rights societies and others for use in specialized search activities.

At the time publication of the *Catalog* was first authorized, in the Act of March 3, 1891, the ostensible purpose was to provide customs officers, and postmasters of post offices receiving foreign mails, with means of preventing the importation into the United States of piratical foreign editions of works under copyright here. There were other motivations, however, that affected the form and content of the *Catalog*. Thorvald Solberg voiced some of them in 1904 (as will be seen, p. 74): to facilitate searches of the record, secure the record against loss or destruction, and make a current record of the literary and artistic production of the United States. Other specific uses of the *Catalog* developed during the years, but only its original purpose continued to be suggested in the law, long after the Treasury Department had made clear that the *Catalog* was not in fact helpful in preventing the importation of piratical works.

Our study necessarily involves the relationship of the *Catalog of Copyright Entries* to other works comparable to it in comprehensiveness or in function. It has been limited, however, to relationships to works produced in the United States. To have attempted a comparison with the many official listings of new intellectual works now produced by the governments of the world would have extended this volume considerably. It is enough to point out that in many countries the preparation of current, comprehensive bibliographies of the national intellectual production is based upon the works received in a national center through the operation of a deposit system (copyright, legal, or voluntary). The degree to which the United States system has been similar or dissimilar to the patterns established in other countries will, it is believed, be evident to many readers.

2 Predecessors of the *Catalog of Copyright Entries*

GENERAL BACKGROUND

While the *Catalog of Copyright Entries* came into being as long ago as 1891, it was not the first published catalog produced in the United States as a direct result of the operation of the copyright law. The first such catalog appeared in the 1820's; a second appeared at mid-century. These early attempts to inaugurate a current comprehensive listing of works of United States origin were to a large extent exploratory, and perhaps lacking in clear-cut objective; for these and other reasons they existed but briefly.

The nation's first copyright law (1790) provided for the deposit of copies. Prior to publication, the deposit and registration of "titles" in the district courts was required; following publication, the deposit of copies of the published works had to be made with the Secretary of State. All subsequent copyright laws have provided for the deposit of copies and registration of claims. Yet it was not until the second half of the century that general compliance with these provisions was achieved.

It is not difficult to understand why this was so. The nation was new, and it was occupied with a wide range of pressing problems. From 1790 through most of the nineteenth century the copyright law pertained principally to the protection of books. In the last years of the century the producers of periodicals, works of art, and music, including spokesmen for the craftsmen involved in the production of these materials, and spokesmen for the public using these materials, were able to bring influence upon copyright legislation. For most of the century, however, the important copyright material was the book, and those who influenced the development of the law were the creators, producers, distributors, and users of books.

Until the nation's break with England there was virtually no American literary movement of consequence. Political independence brought an awareness of the importance of achieving social, economic, and cultural independence as well; the drive to establish a national literature was strong among many of the country's first statesmen. The first copyright law was one result of that interest.

As Rollo Silver notes in Lehmann-Haupt's *The Book in America:* "while, prior to 1820, American creative literature was insignificant, books for American life, such as school texts, theological works, and practical handbooks were an important cultural factor. . . . The significant meaning of the great increase in reading between 1830 and 1840 should also be suggested. The new interest in primary and secondary education created greatly improved schoolbooks. This, too, was the period of the establishment of the Penny Press and of many major periodicals—all influencing the reading habits of the populace. . . . standard works of history, law, medicine, and science . . . appeared between 1800 and 1850. Brilliantly and steadily, throughout these years, scholars prepared and the publishers issued books of importance in national and world culture." [1]

Throughout the nineteenth century Boston, Philadelphia, and New York were active book-publishing centers. By mid-century New York outstripped the other two cities in book production and was taking the leadership in book trade activities. By this time, too, the printer in other smaller cities who had often been a publisher of books as well as of newspapers, had lost opportunity and incentive to publish books, leaving this field, on the whole, to the more specialized book publishers in the three coastal cities. Many of today's book-publishing dynasties were thriving concerns by 1850. During the second half of the century more new publishing houses were established in these and other metropolitan centers. One factor that contributed to increase the distribution of books was technological improvements which reduced the cost of production. Another was the piracy of British books by some American publishers; this was responsible for the agitation which resulted in the so-called "international copyright law" of 1891.[2]

As new publishers were established in various parts of the country, independent booksellers opened stores in population centers to make the books available to the public. The booksellers needed to keep informed about what books were being issued by what publishers. Some periodicals and newspapers, such as *The Port Folio* from 1801 on and *The North American Review* from 1819, regularly carried announcements of new books; but this was not enough. It was the bookseller, rather than the publisher or librarian, who had motivation strong enough to attempt to produce the first book trade bibliographies. The booksellers of Boston were responsible for nonserial bibliographies in 1797 and 1804.[3]

Adolph Growoll tells us that early in the century a New York bookdealer and publisher, Evert Duyckinck, "inaugurated the system of furnishing his customers, booksellers as well as private buyers, with printed lists of the latest books." [4] After his death in 1833 the practice was continued by Orville A. Roorbach, a former clerk in Duyckinck's store. In 1849 Roorbach published the first bibliography of the American book trade worthy of the name, the *Bibliotheca Americana; Catalogue of American Publications.* It listed works published in the United States from 1820 through 1848, and was a compilation of the notes compiled currently over these years. A supplement was issued in 1850. A revision of the original work incorporating the supplementary items collected up to October was published late in 1852.

In 1851 the *Bibliotheca Americana* was supplemented on a current basis by the issues of *Norton's Literary Advertiser.*

Roorbach continued his work on his original plan until the onset of the Civil War, issuing three-year supplements to his 1820-52 volume in 1855, 1858, and 1861. Near the close of the war a clerk in the firm of John Wiley & Son, James Kelly, decided to continue Roorbach's work,[5] and issued two volumes covering five years each, 1861-65 and 1866-70. "Both Roorbach and Kelly," comments Constance Winchell, "are unsatisfactory as they are far from complete and often inaccurate, but they must be used as they are the most general lists for the period 1820-70." [6]

"In January, 1869," writes Growoll, "Frederick Leypoldt, then of the firm of Leypoldt & Holt . . . issued in the 'Annual Number' of *The Literary Bulletin, a Monthly Record of Current Literature,* started in December, 1868, what proved to be the first step towards his 'American Catalogue.'" [7] Leypoldt continued the current compilation of entries; founded *Publishers' Weekly* in 1872; and started the *Publishers' Trade List Annual* in 1873 and the *Library Journal* in 1876 (the year of the organization of the American Library Association). In 1879 Richard Rogers Bowker succeeded Leypoldt in most of these enterprises, including the *American Catalogue.* While this bibliography was superseded by the publications of H. W. Wilson after 1910, the Bowker firm has continued to be the source of the trade information vital to the publisher and bookseller, through weekly lists of new books, with monthly indexes, in *Publishers' Weekly,* and annual compilations of publishers' catalogs in *Publishers' Trade List Annual.* Of late years the latter has been supplemented by *Books in Print* and by the new *Subject Guide to Books in Print.*

These bibliographies all had their origins in the book trade and had as their primary objective service to the book trade. They were confined to new books and books in print, i.e. books presumably available for purchase either in bookstores or at the publishers'. They did not and could not, except in part, serve the interests of the antiquarian book trade, nor of the libraries and scholars searching for older works no longer easily obtainable.

The bibliographical series of greatest significance to libraries in the twentieth century was initially of book trade origin and in fact continues to serve a predominantly trade function. This was the monthly *Cumulative Book Index* begun by a Minneapolis bookdealer, Halsey W. Wilson, in 1898. It was prompted by Mr. Wilson's difficulties in identifying a book when a customer would mention only part of the information required.[8] He provided author, title, and subject entries in one alphabet, and cumulated entries at regular intervals; in this way he achieved a complete, comprehensive listing of American books, while providing a current and constantly up-to-date information service. In addition, at intervals between 1900 and 1928 he issued in the *United States Catalog* comprehensive lists of books in print. These two services were standard bibliographical sources for the book world by 1928, when they were critically described by Van Hoesen as forming "a continuous and fairly complete list of American books." [9]

The bibliographies produced by and for the book trade are of interest in this survey principally because they constitute for some periods the best, and for other periods the only, bibliographical record in existence. They have value today, and will continue to have value in the future, as indication if not proof of the existence of specific works, and as sources of the bibliographical data needed for identification.

In addition to the trade bibliographies, however, comprehensive bibliographies have been compiled which have had a record function as their principal objective. With few exceptions, possible uses members of the book trade might have for these works have not influenced the compilers either in setting up the limitations within which they have worked or in determining the data to be recorded.

The first major effort to make a record of works produced in America was that of Isaiah Thomas, printer-publisher-antiquarian of Worcester, Massachusetts. On April 1, 1808, when he was fifty-nine, Thomas began "writing a Sketch of the Origin and progress of printing." [10] Four weeks later he began compiling a list of the books printed in the colonies up to the time of the Revolutionary War. His *History of Printing in America* was published in 1810, but the planned catalog of titles was not included. He had found not only that a second volume would be required for the list but also that the entries would require a more extensive re-editing than he was prepared to undertake. The publication of the list was therefore deferred.[11]

He saw to it, however, that his notes were preserved, by bequeathing them to the American Antiquarian Society, which he had founded in 1812. "Experience had shown him," wrote his grandson, Benjamin Franklin Thomas, "how quickly the sources of our history were drying up, how rapidly the monuments of the past were crumbling and wasting away. He saw and understood, no man better, from what infinitely varied and minute sources the history of a nation's life was to be drawn; that the only safe rule was to gather up all the fragments so that nothing be lost." [12]

The list finally appeared, after extensive editing by Samuel F. Haven, Jr., under the title "Catalogue of American Publications, 1639-1775," as a 350-page appendix to the second edition of the *History of Printing* published by Joel Munsell at Albany in 1874 for the American Antiquarian Society. With its publication the Society had fulfilled the hope of Isaiah Thomas to produce "the only Catalogue of (early) American printed books, of any consequence, or in any way general, to be met with, or that has been made." [13] It is interesting to note that Isaiah Thomas had identified approximately eight thousand titles for the period 1639-1775, inclusive.

The interest of Isaiah Thomas was essentially antiquarian, and the intent of his work was to preserve for future times the record of the past. This was also the primary incentive of Charles Evans in traversing the same ground nearly a hundred years later. Evans, a librarian with an intense interest in American publishing, devoted the years of his retirement to an exhaustive compilation, chronologically arranged, containing full descriptions of the works printed in the United States from the beginning in 1639. He did not achieve his intended final date of 1820; the work was concluded at 1800 by another compiler. Evans' twelve-volume *American Bibliography*, privately published between 1903 and 1934, is described by Winchell as "the most important general list of early American publications, indispensable in the large reference or special library." Wherever possible he included locations of copies, "an especially important feature."[14] He also included details of the facts of copyright registration for many works issued between 1790 and 1800, and must have had access to the copyright record books of the Department of State and of the Pennsylvania District Court.[15]

The antiquarian interests of a London bookseller, Obadiah Rich, together with the growing prospects of sales to American collectors and libraries, led to his compiling sales catalogs of books relating to America. These catalogs were of more than ordinary interest as bibliographies since they were arranged chronologically by the year in which the works were printed. The first one, *A Catalogue of Books, Relating Principally to America,* covering the sixteenth and seventeenth centuries, was issued in 1832. In 1835, 1841, and 1846 Rich supplemented this with issues of his *Bibliotheca Americana Nova* covering the eighteenth and nineteenth centuries to 1846. At the time the record value of these catalogs was substantial, although it is clear enough that Rich's principal purpose in issuing them was to sell books. The Library of Congress, at any rate, bought extensively from him in the 1840's.[16]

The same concept was engaging the attention of another bookman about the same time. This was Henry Stevens, a roving agent for a number of wealthy American collectors, including Peter Force. Stevens tentatively arranged for the preparation of "Bibliographia Americana: A Bibliographical Account of the Sources of American History; comprising a description of books relating to America, printed prior to the year 1700, and of all books printed in America from 1543 to 1700," to be published by the Smithsonian Institution.[17] The work was never completed. It is interesting to note, in passing, that the Joint Committee on the Library of Congress authorized the subscription of $250 to the project on August 5, 1848.[18]

It was also in 1848 that Joseph Sabin came to the United States from England and began working as a salesman and cataloger for George S. Appleton in Philadelphia.[19] Almost immediately he began compilation of the entries subsequently published between 1868 and 1936 as the 29-volume *Bibliotheca Americana, A Dictionary of Books Relating to America, From Its Discovery to the Present Time.* Sabin did not live long enough to see the work through to completion—other hands took up this task; nevertheless, he had performed the larger part of the work singlehanded as a by-product of his daily activities in the book trade. The location of copies in libraries was given when known.[20]

In addition to these major efforts to record, in bibliographic terms, the products of the young nation's creativeness, there were hundreds of minor projects of similar nature but of more limited objective. Catalogs promoting the sales of books, catalogs indexing the contents of libraries for the use of readers, and bibliographies of individual writers and of special subjects for the assistance of scholars were issued in quantity. The primary incentives for the production of comprehensive catalogs, pretending to substantial completeness, were two: to facilitate the distribution of books by sale, and to provide a definitive record.

ELLIOT'S LIST OF PATENTS GRANTED BY THE UNITED STATES

As has been shown, the interest of the trade bibliographers was in the current compilation of lists of currently produced works, in order to facilitate their sale. The concept of current compilation for record purposes rather than trade uses was first developed in Washington as a direct result of the section of the copyright law providing for the deposit of copies. The records maintained by the Department of State were records of works deposited and therefore are reliable evidence that the works recorded did actually exist in at least one copy on the date of record. The district court records, on the other hand, were records of the deposit of titles before publication and thus included notices of some projected publications which never actually were published. The first works received by the Secretary of State were recorded in 1796.[1] The deposit copy continued to go to the Department of State as a matter of law until 1859 (deposits after 1831 being made to the district courts and forwarded at least once a year to the Secretary of State); it went to the Department of the Interior until 1870. An additional deposit copy was required to be sent to the Smithsonian Institution from 1846 to 1859, and one to the Library of Congress from 1846 to 1859 and from 1865 to 1870. Since 1870 the Library of Congress has received all deposit copies required by the law, either one or two depending upon the classification of the work.

The first published catalog of works resulting from the operation of the copyright law was a thirteen-page appendix to the 1822 issue of an anonymously compiled serial, *A List of Patents Granted by the United States,* first brought out in 1820.[2] The copyright notice states that a copy of the title of *A List of Patents* was deposited with the clerk of the district court on July 25, 1820. Supplements were issued in 1822 and annually through 1826, in a form intended for addition to and to be bound with the 1796-1820 main section. New title pages were printed to show additions and changes in content, and in 1822 what appears to be merely a variant title page—*American Museum, and Repository of Arts and Sciences*—was included. In 1828 the supplements were cumulated into the main list. This list, printed from the same type, formed the main section of William Elliot's *Patentee's Manual* (1830).[3]

The catalog was not an impressive work even in its day. Fortunately the motivations which produced it can be identified, and these have a relationship to the problem to which this book is addressed. In order to place the catalog in its proper setting it is necessary to review briefly certain developments in operations under the patent law.

The Department of State at this time had relatively little to do with the formulation of foreign policy; it was the communications center for American ministers and consuls abroad and for foreign ministers residing in Washington, and was responsible for issuing passports and handling other matters concerning Americans beyond the shores of the United States. It also had responsibility for a miscellany of internal activities: publication of the laws, maintenance of the departmental library, recommendations to the President on pardons and claims, supervision of the census, and the "almost independent" work involved in the granting of patents. Both patents and copyright deposits were in the jurisdiction of the Secretary of State[4] for many years: patents from 1790 to 1849 and copyright deposits until 1859. Initially, patents were granted by a Patent Board consisting of the Secretary of State, Secretary of War, and the Attorney General; in 1793 the Board was abolished.[5] Clerks of the State Department handled the granting of patents and recordation of copyright deposits until 1802. In 1801 the patent work was physically removed from the quarters occupied by the State Department; for various reasons—chiefly the space requirements of the patent work and its unique nature—it has been separately housed since then.

In 1802 James Madison, then Secretary of State, put his friend, the "many-sided near-genius"[6] William Thornton, in charge of issuing patents. Thornton was a remarkable man on many counts, but is perhaps best remembered as the original designer of the Capitol building. For most of his tenure he ran a one- or two-man patent operation, lacking the distinction even of a title. Soon after 1810 he gave himself the title "Superintendent of Patents." Not unnaturally, he had little interference from above. This was undoubtedly most satisfactory to a man inclined to independence, and since his integrity and dedication were unquestioned and the work ran quietly on the whole, he was able to handle his modest workload in his own way.

That it was modest is illustrated by the fact that in 1805, for example, 57 patents were granted and 40 copyright deposits recorded; in 1810, 223 patents and 19 deposits; in 1815, 173 patents and 13 deposits; in 1820, 150 patents and 40 deposits.[7] Nevertheless, at least by 1817, he had one assistant, and was beginning to have his troubles. When one discontented inventor laid his case before Secretary of State John Quincy Adams, and the Secretary asked for an explanation, Thornton replied, December 13, 1817: "I am not unaccustomed to the railings of the disappointed, but I feel so perfectly confident of the correctness of my proceedings, that they produce no impression upon me. I have desired Mr. Elliot, who is the only clerk in my office, and in whose integrity and honor I have the utmost confidence, to wait on you, and explain my conduct. I thought it better than to do it myself, as you will be so good as to question him freely respecting me, and if you wish any further explanation from me I will do myself the honor of waiting on you at any moment. I have hopes if there be a purgatory, that the Superintendent of the Patent Office will be exempt from many sufferings in consequence of the dire Situation he has experienced on Earth." [8]

The clerk mentioned may have been either William Elliot or Seth Alfred Elliot, both of whom were employed by Dr. Thornton, William Elliot certainly by 1817 and Seth Alfred apparently by 1820. It is more likely that it was William Elliot who had acquired this degree of trust, since he appears most prominently in later accounts of patent and copyright matters. He had been a teacher of mathematics in England before he came to America early in the 1800's.[9] He established the *Washington City Gazette* in 1813 in support of the Republican party, employing as editor George Watterston,[10] who became first Librarian of Congress on March 21, 1815. Elliot, at least by 1817, became the clerk of Dr. Thornton and was ultimately to be called the "first clerk" [11] in the Patent Office. His intellectual pursuits were varied and included active participation in the work of the Washington Botanical Society, of which he was one of the founding members (1817). In 1821 he assisted William Lambert, a clerk in the pension office, in making the observations required to establish the exact latitude and longitude of Washington.[12]

The publication for which he is best known was *The Washington Guide,* first issued in 1822 and frequently revised and reissued.[13] The *Guide* contained an odd assortment of information, with a relatively large amount of space devoted to the operation of the patent law. William Elliot left the Patent Office in 1829[14] and served as surveyor of the City of Washington from 1832 to 1835.[15]

Seth Alfred Elliot, a printer by trade,[16] was associated with William Elliot as printer-publisher of *The Washington Guide* and in other activities.

It is apparent that both William and Seth Alfred recognized that the Government was a source of information of value to the public and that the regular recording activities provided by law made Washington the national source of such information.

Beginning in 1805 the Secretary of State was required to publish lists of the patents granted. A second list appeared in 1811, and thereafter supplements were issued annually. Until about 1831, when initial steps were taken to classify patents, they were listed in chronological order by the date granted, with the title of the invention as recorded and the name of the inventor. The patents were not numbered and there were no indexes in the published records. Obviously, except for scanning for information as each new list appeared, these lists were difficult to use, particularly as the numbers of patents increased.[17]

William Elliot evidently believed this was not enough, even though it was probably one of his responsibilities under Dr. Thornton to prepare the lists for publication. On November 24, 1819, he wrote to his superior, thanking him for having mentioned to Secretary of State Adams a project "to publish a work similar to the 'Repertory of Arts,' [18] published in England." He concluded: "Subscription papers and proposals for this purpose have been issued more than a year:—and I have no doubt when the Ho. Sec'y understands these facts he will promote our undertaking." [19]

In the following year Seth Alfred Elliot, evidently then also on the staff of Dr. Thornton, wrote from the "Patent Office," August 11, to Daniel Brent, chief clerk[20] of the Department of State, requesting him to obtain "the Secretary of State's answer to my proposal requesting the purchase of the pamphlet containing an Alphabetical List of Patents granted for the last 30 years. . . . I would be glad to receive an early answer, so that if they are not purchased, I may take measures to dispose of them."[21]

The work referred to in this letter is unquestionably the *List of Patents Granted by the United States,* which Seth Alfred Elliot had just printed, dated July 20, 1820, and which by 1830 would become *The Patentee's Manual,* with authorship clearly credited to William Elliot.[22]

Beginning with the 1822 issue, this work contained an appendix entitled at first "A List of All the Books that have been deposited in the Department of State, for securing their copy right according to law." The arrangement of entries for these works was chronological by the date of the corresponding entry in the record books of the Department of State and consisted of the title of the work, usually shortened, the name of the proprietor or author, and the date the work was recorded.

The annual supplements kept this appendix up to date through May 1825 but it was omitted from later issues of the patent list. A careful check of the content of these lists of deposits against the original record books might reveal some discrepancies; they profess, however, to contain all the deposits received by the Department of State between 1796 and May 1825, a period of nearly thirty years. The titles of approximately 950 works, largely books, but also a few maps, charts, prints, and musical compositions, are recorded in them.[22] The following are typical entries:

American Cookery, &c. by Amelia Simmons, May 26th, 1796.

American Biography, or an Historical account of those persons who have been distinguished in America, by Je. Belknap, D.D. Dec. 12th, 1798.

The New American Practical Navigator—by Nathaniel Bowditch, March 5th, 1802.

A Map of the United States, &c. by Abraham Bradley, jr. Apl. 26th, 1796.

Ellen Arise, a Ballad, written by J. E. Harwood—Composed by B. Can [i.e. Carr], June 30th, 1798.

An engraving of the Rev. John Carroll, D.D. by Benj. Tanner, Sept. 28, do [i.e. 1812].

By almost any standards this was an elementary—one might say primitive—effort to provide information. The order in which the works were recorded in the Department of State largely determined the order of listing in the publication. Because of the small number of deposits in these years and because the deposits were omitted from the Secretary of State's annual letter listing patents, it apparently was thought there was no need to undertake anything more elaborate.

This was not the case, however, with the list of patents. As mentioned before, the published patent lists of the Secretary of State were confined to a straight chronological listing. The Elliot publication made two principal improvements. While it maintained at first a basically chronological order, it improved upon this by inverting titles to bring the significant word first so that if there were two or more inventions involving water wheels in the same month they would fall together in the list and so facilitate use. And it provided an alphabetical list of patentees.

In urging the purchase of his first list by the Secretary of State, Seth Alfred Elliot in his letter of August 11, 1820, stated the objectives of the work:

"By this book three important points of information to the public are obtained; and which are, in some degree, connected with the Laws of the United States.

"1st—An inventor will see what *is patented* on the subject of his invention, and will be enabled to decide with more certainty, whether he be or not, an original inventor.

"2d—The public will know what *is*, or *is not, patented;* which will prevent many impositions.

"3d—The public will know when patents *expire.*"

This statement makes clear that in Seth Alfred Elliot's mind, at least, the list contributed information to inventors for their protection, and to the public both for its protection and to enable it to know when a patent would fall in the public domain. While he had improved somewhat upon the State Department's method of listing patents, he was unable to secure the Secretary's assent to his proposition. To a degree, however, the lists anticipated and probably hastened the eventual adoption of a classification system by the Patent Office.

Dr. Thornton died in 1828 and was succeeded by John D. Craig. In 1829 Martin Van Buren became Secretary of State and almost immediately ordered Craig to conduct an investigation into the causes of discrepancies between the numbers of patents granted and the fees deposited with the Treasury. In response to Craig's request for information William Elliot, in a letter dated January 16, 1830,[23] reviewed Dr. Thornton's practices in some detail. While Elliot's explanations failed to satisfy Craig in every particular, no action was taken against him; however, a tightening up of the fiscal operations of the Patent Office was a direct result.

Only when William Elliot was no longer in the Patent Office was his name included, in the 1830 issue, as compiler of the lists of patents published by Seth Alfred Elliot. Nevertheless there can be no doubt that he was involved in their compilation. Examination of the copyright record books maintained by the Department of State suggests this to be true since many entries were signed by William Elliot. The copyright entries in the published lists were in the same order as those in the record book and contain no information not recorded there; the information is given in the same sequence, but in somewhat abbreviated form.

While William Elliot was not officially connected with the Department of State after 1829 he evidently continued to believe there was a public need for lists of copyright deposits. When *Wheaton* vs. *Peters* focused attention on the effect of failure to deposit copies, Elliot's cause was supported by a communication signed "Cadmus" addressed "To Authors" which appeared in the *National Intelligencer* of March 24, 1834:

"About two years ago, Mr. Wm. Elliot, of Washington, for many years first clerk in the Patent Office, made out a list of all the books deposited for copy right in the Department of State, for forty years—alphabetically and analogically arranged;

—but, owing to the manner in which he was treated by Congress respecting his List of Patents [presumably his *Patentee's Manual* of 1830], and legal decisions thereon (Congress having reprinted the work without compensation to the proprietor,) he has declined publishing it, and it therefore remains still in manuscript, he fearing that in case he should publish it, he might again experience the same treatment.

"A memorial on this subject has been before the Judiciary Committee of the House of Representatives for the two last sessions. As this work, from the late decision of the Supreme Court, would be highly interesting to the public, it is to be hoped Congress will do justice to all parties, by publishing the work in question without further delay."

On December 16 of the same year, W. D. Johnston writes in his *History of the Library of Congress*, "Mr. Robbins [Asher Robbins of Rhode Island?] presented to the Senate a petition praying for the patronage of Congress in the publication of the work; but the Library Committee to whom the petition had been referred, voted, January 31, 1835, that a motion be made to discharge the committee from its further consideration." [24]

So far as is known, Elliot did not again propose the publication of his list of copyright deposits. But he was not yet ready to give up with respect to his list of patents. An extensive revision of the patent law, the Act of July 4, 1836, created the Patent Office, still within the Department of State, and made detailed provisions for the improvement of facilities for examining and registering patents and maintaining the models and records, including provisions for a new Patent Office building. It was too late: on December 15, 1836, the Patent Office was destroyed by fire, its estimated 7,000 models, 9,000 drawings, and 230 books along with it.

William Elliot promptly brought out a new edition of his *Guide*, in which he wrote eloquently of the nation's loss:

"When we look upon the dreadful ruin spread around by the destruction of the archives of the patent-office, the most solemn feeling must overwhelm the mind. There lie the ashes of the records of more than ten thousand inventions, with their beautiful models and drawings. There lie, also, smouldering in the same heap of ruins, the elegant and classic correspondence of Dr. Thornton, with most of the ingenious and scientific men of this country and of Europe, for upwards of twenty-three years.

"To remedy as far as possible this appalling disaster, it is recommended that a complete list of all the patents that have been granted by the United States since 1790, till the present time, be published by the Government, (which the writer of this article could furnish;) arranged analogically and chronologically as regards the subjects, and alphabetically as regards the names of the patentees. Also, a complete copy of all the patent laws, with the legal decisions which have taken place under them. This work would make two volumes 8vo. of about 400 or 500 pages each, and be like a dictionary, of ready and easy reference; and in no respect like the imperfect and unintelligible list published, some years since, by Congress."

Thirty-five years ahead of his time he foresaw the kind of publication needed in the public interest.

"It is suggested that the specifications of all the patents hereafter granted, be printed and distributed like the laws of the United States. This system would not only prevent them from being lost and impaired, but would give much general and useful information, and would prevent many impositions on the public. W.E." [25]

The Patent Office fire had provided another selling point—safety of the record—but it was not enough. Congress was too little interested, and had too little money to devote to such specialized projects. So the first lists of patents and of works deposited under the United States copyright law to be published in a form designed for use by the public were produced by private funds, though upon the initiative and through the enterprise of a government employee who had come to believe in the soundness of producing informational works for the public at the seat of government where the official records were made. It would appear that his publishing experience had demonstrated the need for government financial support of such projects; at any rate, he had endeavored to secure such support over a period of eighteen years, but without success.

JEWETT'S "COPY-RIGHT PUBLICATIONS"

Elliot's idea of a currently compiled published record of United States works was taken up a few years later by the far-seeing librarian of the new Smithsonian Institution and became a basic element of the many-faceted bibliographical program which he was to develop and promote with vigor and persistence. This librarian was Charles Coffin Jewett of Brown University, who accepted the position of assistant secretary and librarian of the Smithsonian on February 11, 1847,[1] six months after the Institution was established by the Act of August 10, 1846. This act also directed the authors and proprietors of copyright works to deposit copies with the Smithsonian Institution and the Library of Congress[2] in addition to the copy required for eventual deposit with the Secretary of State.

While Jewett did not enter upon full-time service at the Smithsonian until January 1, 1849,[3] he devoted much of his thinking, after accepting the position nearly two years earlier, to the opportunities and problems which lay before him. He did not hesitate, before leaving Brown, to present to his superior, Joseph Henry, Secretary of the Institution, his views on topics of concern to him. For instance, he wrote to Henry "in the late fall of 1847," according to his biographer Borome, advising that "immediate steps be taken to see that the Institution should receive the books to which it was entitled under the copyright section of the 1846 law." [4] He chafed under the knowledge that the absence of penalties for failure to deposit was responsible for the small degree of compliance with this provision, and on April 26, 1848, wrote a long letter to Henry urging congressional action to correct the situation. He stated his position clearly: "If it be considered just and expedient to require three copies of every book, let the delivery of them be made obligatory and essential to the securing of a valid title. I have always thought that at least *two* copies should be required, because there is always danger of losing one by fire or otherwise. One of these copies should be kept in a safe depository, from *which it should never be taken,* except by order of a Court of Law." [5]

Jewett was interested in the deposit of copies not only as a means of building up the Smithsonian library but also as the basis for attaining a current, complete national bibliography; he believed copyright deposit to be the means needed "to provide complete bibliographical control of man's record currently produced within a given nation." [6] National bibliographical enterprise was engaging the attention of many in the book world at this time. Roorbach was ready to publish his trade list, Sabin was about to begin his long task of retrospective compilation, Rich was acquiring and issuing catalogs of Americana, and Henry Stevens (with the blessing of Jewett, Peter Force, and many others) was taking subscriptions to his proposed *Bibliographia Americana.* Jewett was scholar and antiquarian enough to appreciate the value of early records and at the same time was practical enough to see the usefulness, for both current and retrospective uses, of descriptions of works currently compiled. He considered the compilation of such a record to be one of the responsibilities of his position, and in his annual report for 1849 he outlined in some detail the publication he visualized.

"I beg leave to suggest the establishment of a *monthly bulletin,* in which the list of *all works received during the preceding month, with the titles in full, the date of deposit, and the name of the proprietor,* [emphasis supplied] should be printed. Copies of this might be sent to every publisher who complies with the law. This journal might be widely and gratuitously distributed among the literary institutions of this country, and of Europe. The record would then be, as an advertisement, far more valuable to the proprietor than the book sent and the expense of transmission. Although I suggest the commencement of a bulletin in this particular connexion, I would not by any means confine it to the publication of the lists of copyright works. It might include a *scientific* as well as a bibliographical department.

"In the bibliographical department might be published: 1st.

Lists of publications deposited for the security of the copyright; 2d. Lists of accessions to the library and other collections, with the names of donors; 3d. Lists of new works published in Europe; 4th. The contents of the current numbers of the most important reviews and journals in this country and Europe, translating the titles of articles published in other languages than English; 5th. Items of intelligence and short essays of interest to book producers and readers.

"This bulletin might at first be published at irregular intervals, as we find the materials, and it should be of such a general character as not to conflict with any established journal." [7]

He made the suggestion a reality to the extent of causing lists of deposited copyrighted works to be added, under the heading "Copy-right Publications," in two appendices to the report of the Smithsonian Institution for the year 1850.[8] While this was the only part of Jewett's proposed bibliographical bulletin that was achieved, it deserves attention as the second precursor of the *Catalog of Copyright Entries*. Like those issued by Elliot, these lists were of works deposited in copies, not simply of works registered.

The first appendix contained entries for works deposited prior to 1850; the second, for works deposited during 1850. Each appendix was divided into three parts: books; musical compositions; and "maps, charts, prints and labels." Each part was arranged alphabetically by author, when available from the work, or by title. The arrangement of several works of one author under his name follows no apparent alphabetical or chronological order.

The entries were relatively full. Authors' names apparently were given in the form in which they appeared in their books, including their degrees and learned society affiliations if supplied. Titles were transcribed in full, with alternative titles and subtitles, followed by an edition statement when given on the title page, size, number of pages, place of publication, publisher, and year of publication when given on the title page; the final item was the name of the person or corporate body who sent in the deposit. The music entry included medium of performance when given on the title page. Beginning with entries of 1849 for music and the 1850 entries for books, the day, month, and year of the deposit were added following the depositor's name. The relatively brief entries for maps, charts, prints, and labels included a characterization of the physical nature of the work where this was not obvious from the title; e.g. sheet, chart, label, and, where appropriate, such statements as "in raised letters for the use of the blind."

The following typical examples demonstrate the fullness of the entries:

Irving (Washington) Oliver Goldsmith: a biography. By Washington Irving, [being, as by first title page, Vol. 11 of] The Works of Washington Irving. New edition, revised: 12mo 383p—New York, published by George P. Putnam, 1850; deposited by W. Irving, 20 August 1850.

Fillmore (Augustus D.) Our old Homestead. Words by Miss Phoebe Cary. Music composed by A. D. Fillmore: 4to 3p —Cincinnati, published by D. Anderson, 1850; deposited by D. Anderson, 9 November, 1850.

Doty (H. H.) Susannah and the Elders: drawn on stone by N. Sarony; the original by Louis Blanc—Philadelphia, published by H. H. Doty, 1849; deposited by H. H. Doty.

In his report for 1850 Jewett indicated that receipts of copyright deposits from 1846 through 1850 totaled 2,057 items.[9] This presumably is the number of works or pieces represented in his catalog of copyright deposits.

Deposits were also being received after August 10, 1846, by the Library of Congress. The first ones were noted in the Letter Book for 1843-1849 on October 19, 1846: Samuel Alsop, *An Elementary Treatise on Algebra,* and William Vogdes, *An Elementary Treatise on Mensuration,* both published in Philadelphia in 1846 by E. C. & J. Biddle. The Library also took pains to publish at least partial lists of them, not as a contribution to national bibliography, which was Jewett's approach, but simply as additions to the collections. Like most other large American libraries in this period, the Library of Congress issued printed catalogs of its holdings. The plan of publication at this time was to issue a complete catalog at ten-year intervals, with annual supplements listing the additions of that year. In the 1846 supplement to the catalog there appeared for the first time a brief section with this heading: "Received in compliance with the 10th section of the 'Act to establish the Smithsonian Institution.'"[10] Fourteen works were briefly listed in this, the Library's first published record of copyright deposits. The extreme brevity of the entries is illustrated by those for the first two deposits received:

Chapter	No.	
25	15*a*	Alsop on Algebra, 12 mo.
26	1*b*	Vogdes on Mensuration and Geometry, 12 mo.

These lists of copyright receipts were cumulated in the 1847 and 1848 supplements, and the receipts of law books by copyright deposit were listed separately. The separate listing of copyright deposits was discontinued in the next complete catalog, that for 1849. In this catalog entries for works received by copyright were interfiled with those received by other means but were distinguished by a double dagger placed at the end of the entry. This was a classed catalog containing location symbols; the bibliographic entry included, in this order, author, full title, size, place of publication, and date of publication. Here is an entry on page 667:

Chapter XXV. Mathematics—Pure. Arithmetic.
15*a*—Alsop, Samuel: Elementary Treatise on Algebra, in which the Principles of the Science are familiarly Explained, and Illustrated by numerous Examples, 12. mo.; Philadelphia, 1846.‡

Copyright deposits continued to be distinguished by the double dagger in certain of the annual supplements and in the complete catalog issued in 1861 containing entries for works received through 1859. Then the Act of February 5, 1859,[11] shut off the flow of copyright deposits to both the Smithsonian and the Library of Congress, as we shall see.

Librarian of Congress Meehan was concerned about serving the needs of the Congress; Librarian of the Smithsonian Jewett, on the other hand, visualized the function of his library both as a center of research in all fields and as a national agency having responsibility for the coordination of national bibliographical activities. Jewett's annual reports between 1849 and 1853 contain long expositions of the merits of his plans and proposals. In addition to his proposed monthly bulletin listing new publications, and an improved plan for securing the prompt deposit of the copyrighted books, without which the catalog could not exist, he planned to develop a cataloging code for the United States using Antonio Panizzi's rules for the British Museum as a basis, publish guides to the library resources of the nation, develop an interlibrary loan system, and publish a national union catalog through the use of stereotyped catalog entries. He even tentatively advanced the idea of an international copyright exchange:

"If . . . a duplicate collection of all works for which copyrights are secured in this country could be made, it might be offered to England in exchange for a like collection of its own publications; and this exchange, if prosperous between two countries, might be extended to all the principal nations of the book-making world. . . .

"Nothing, it seems to me, could more effectually conduce to the rapid progress of science and humanity, than a system which should make the literary and scientific labors in each country known immediately in all others." [12]

Differences in point of view developed between Jewett and Secretary Henry of the Smithsonian, however, and the copyright deposit system was a principal cause of the friction. By

1851 Secretary Henry began to express serious reservations about copyright deposits in his annual report. He was willing to grant that while a copy of "every book originally published in this country should be somewhere preserved, it does not follow that the Smithsonian fund ought to be burdened with the expense of this charge." In his view the great majority of the books received were "such as are found in almost every public and private library; but very few of them would ever be purchased by the Institution, and are consequently dear at any price." [13]

Jewett continued to expound the value of the deposit system to the national (i.e. Smithsonian) library, dwelling upon its advantages time after time. "If we had means . . . of forming a complete collection of copyright works, we would reject nothing, not even that which might, to ourselves, appear utterly trivial and unworthy of preservation." [14] As far as Secretary Henry was concerned, however, the national library and national bibliographical center concept had grown out of bounds.

Relations between the two men deteriorated until "a difficulty" occurred which led to Jewett's "separation from the Institution" on or about July 10, 1854.[15] Henry continued to press for relief from the flow of deposits. While he recognized that the law "was intended to benefit the Institution," he considered the effect to be the reverse: "The articles received are principally elementary school manuals and the ephemeral productions of the teeming press, including labels for patent medicines, perfumery, and sheets of popular music. The cost of postage, clerk-hire, certificates, shelf-room, etc., of these far exceeds the value of the good works received. Indeed, all the books published in the United States, which might be required for the Library, could have been purchased for one-tenth of what has been expended on those obtained by the copyright law. Similar complaints are made by the Library of Congress and the Department of State . . ." [16] The receipt of 848 separate pieces of music in 1854, more than half of all the copyright deposits received in that year, was more than he could bear, and quite enough to demonstrate to him "that the operation of the present copyright law does not confer a material benefit on the Institution . . ." [17]

Kathrine Oliver Murra summarizes Jewett's contributions to bibliographic planning as follows: "His plan contained three points basic to an investigation and understanding of the concept of current complete national bibliography: (a) adaptation of a new technique for rapidly and less-expensively producing a catalog of bibliographical entries—stereotyping; (b) cooperation of those bodies best qualified to provide the segments of a complete listing—the public libraries; (c) improvement of the *most logical channel through which the major part of man's record as currently published in the United States* could be obtained for listing—copyright registration." (Emphasis supplied.) She gives as reasons for Jewett's failure: there were "mechanical defects" in the stereotype process; "cooperative activity was a faltering business"; and "the copyright system directed a stream of materials to the Smithsonian Library which it was both unable for lack of funds and unwilling because of the nature of the materials received to catalog." [18] Jewett left the Smithsonian to become superintendent of the Boston Public Library.

Responsibility for copyright matters was finally, after nearly seventy years, transferred from the State Department to the Department of the Interior by the Act of February 5, 1859,[19] ten years after the patent work had been similarly transferred. In Interior, copyright affairs became a responsibility of the Commissioner of Patents, who appointed a "librarian of copyrights" to handle the work. The law effecting this transfer also removed the requirement of the deposit of copies with the Smithsonian Institution and the Library of Congress, confining the deposit requirement to the one copy now to be deposited after publication with the Secretary of the Interior.

The role of the Smithsonian Institution during the period of the deposit of copies there and in the Library of Congress between 1846 and 1859 had been outstanding largely because of the work of Charles Coffin Jewett. The Librarian of Congress during this period, John S. Meehan, had performed his duties conscientiously and methodically but evidently without anything like the far-ranging vision of his contemporary. The disastrous fire at the Library of Congress on Christmas Eve, 1851, had wiped out the major portion of the collection, including a large part of the Jefferson Library and most of the copyright deposits received since 1846. Law was the most important of the major disciplines to be spared. Thirty-five thousand of the Library's 55,000 books had been destroyed, and Mr. Meehan had a major replacement task on his hands. Even so, he demonstrated relatively little interest in the copyright deposits that continued to come in.[20]

With the onset of the Civil War, President Lincoln felt he had reason to remove Meehan from office; this was done on May 24, 1861. Lincoln appointed John G. Stephenson to succeed Meehan. Ainsworth Rand Spofford became first assistant librarian the same year. Stephenson was on active military duty throughout most of his term as librarian, and left the operation of the Library in the hands of Spofford and his assistants.[21]

The "first fruits of the service of Mr. Spofford," as W. D. Johnston records,[22] was the publication of the Library's first alphabetic author catalog, which in its preface gave form to a basic truth: "In the arrangement of any catalogue of books, the chief desideratum, next to accuracy of description, is facility of reference, and to this end all minor considerations should be sacrificed." To make plain that the catalog was only a part of a larger unit, the preface added: "To complete the plan adopted, the present alphabetical catalogue of authors will soon be followed by an analytical catalogue of subjects, also arranged alphabetically." [23] The seeds planted by Jewett were beginning to bear fruit, but in the Library of Congress rather than in the Smithsonian Institution.

3 The Act of March 3, 1891

UNDERLYING BIBLIOGRAPHICAL AND TRADE MOTIVATIONS

Ainsworth Rand Spofford became Librarian of Congress on the last day of the year 1864.[1] To a considerable degree the mantle of Charles Coffin Jewett fell on his shoulders, but he worked in circumstances somewhat more friendly to purposes both held in common. High among the satisfactions of his long service as Librarian and, after 1897, as Chief Assistant Librarian, must have been the passage, after a long struggle, of the so-called "international copyright law," the Act of March 3, 1891.

Secretary Henry of the Smithsonian Institution, while he no longer received new copyright publications, was still burdened by the "general" works acquired, by copyright and otherwise, during Jewett's tenure. He wished to be rid of them. A serious fire in the Smithsonian (within a month after Spofford became Librarian of Congress) gave him added incentive to action, even though the fire had not touched the library. Fortunately "the new Librarian of Congress . . . wanted a National Library as badly as the secretary of the Smithsonian did not want one," the annual report of the Library for 1946 records. "Within . . . sixty-four days [after Spofford's appointment] the Library [of Congress] took a longer step toward its ultimate position among the libraries of the Nation and the world than it had in the sixty-four years since its foundation. . . . This forward movement was effected by two acts passed in the closing days of the session of Congress which opened before Spofford was appointed, on December 5, 1864, and was adjourned on March 3, 1865—the last day of President Lincoln's first term."[2] The first of these, passed on March 2, 1865, provided funds that would soon nearly triple the Library's shelf space. Spofford was receptive to the prospect of a transferral of the Smithsonian library to the Library of Congress. With ample space provided for, negotiations between the two institutions went forward rapidly and were finally consummated on April 5, 1866.[3]

The second act, passed on March 3,[4] reinstated the Library of Congress as recipient of deposits of copyright works in addition to those required to be deposited at this time with the Department of the Interior for completion of the copyright. It provided free mailing privileges for deposit copies and a penalty for the nondeposit of copies; it further specified that the copies sent to the Library should be for the "use" of the Library. To quote the annual report for 1946 further: "Hereby was begun the perfection of the law of copyright in the interest of the National Library which would soon give it its most important means of regular and automatic accumulation, and constitute *the very basis of its unique and national status.* (Emphasis supplied.) These two enactments ushered in the *lustrum mirabile* of the Library of Congress, the extraordinary expansion, consolidation and reconstitution of 1865-70. In the number of books alone the increase of these five years was startling: at the beginning, 82,000 volumes; at their end, 237,000 . . ." [5]

Circumstances were propitious for making further advances. First steps to set up a system of document exchange with foreign governments were taken in 1867 and 1868; while years were to elapse before the system approached perfection, quantities of foreign documents began arriving almost immediately.[6] And the Act of July 8, 1870,[7] transferred to the Library of Congress sole responsibility for administration of the copyright law, including the registry system and the handling of all deposits required by the law. Thus, "by 1870 the future was in large measure provided for, so that the Library would automatically receive, through copyright and document exchange, a great proportion of the world's current literary production, and might henceforth devote its appropriation for increase to filling gaps, acquiring rarities, and rounding out the collections." [8]

Twenty years later Ainsworth Rand Spofford had opportunity to review the objectives of the provisions of the 1870 law and to assess the results:

"The law of copyright, as codified by act of July 8, 1870, made an epoch in the copyright system of the United States. It transferred the entire registry of books and other publications, under copyright law, to the city of Washington, and made the Librarian of Congress sole register of copyrights, instead of the clerks of the District Courts of the United States. Manifold reasons existed for this radical change, and those which were most influential with Congress in making it were the following:

"1. The transfer of the copyright records to Washington it was foreseen would concentrate and simplify the business, and this was a cardinal point. . . . Next, the books would be received at Washington while fresh from the press, instead of, as formerly, several months after issue, or not at all. Then the copyright records would be constantly at hand, where the publications to which they relate were deposited. This would simplify and facilitate reference to the greatest possible degree. . . .

"2. The advantage of securing to our national library a complete collection of all American copyright publications can scarcely be over-estimated. . . . We ought to have one comprehensive library in the country, and that belonging to the nation, whose aim it should be to preserve the books which other libraries have not the room nor the means to procure.

"3. This consideration assumes additional weight when it is remembered that the Library of Congress is freely open to the public throughout the year, and is rapidly becoming the great reference library of the country, resorted to not only by the Congress and the residents of Washington, but by students and writers from all parts of the Union, in search of references and authorities not elsewhere to be found. . . . Its complete catalogue system lends an additional value to its stores. . . .

"4. It was urged with reason that the proposed reform of the unsatisfactory methods of recording and perfecting copyrights would take away the objections so freely brought against the law. . . . [Authors and publishers were put to much trouble and expense] to secure a privilege of uncertain value. [The system fostered errors and omissions which invalidated many copyrights: for example, neglect to deposit with the District Courts, failure by the Court clerks to make a perfect record, neglect to send a second copy for deposit in the Library of Congress, unavailability of the deposits in the District Courts and in the Patent Office.]

"5. The proposed change, it was urged, would be a great economy for the government. It saved the Patent Office the trouble, expense and room of providing for a great library of material which it could not use and did not want. . . . A copyright . . . is not material, but intellectual, and has no natural relation to a department which is charged with the care of the mechanic arts; and it belongs rather to a national library system than to any other department of the civil service. . . .

"By the enactment of the statute of 1870 all the defects in the methods of registration and deposit of copies were obviated. The original records of copyright in all the States were transferred to Washington, and all records of copyright entry were thenceforward kept in the office of the Librarian of Congress. All questions as to literary property, involving a search of records to determine points of validity, such as priority of entry, names of actual owners, transfers or assignments, timely deposit of the required copies, etc., could be determined upon inquiry at a single office of record. These inquiries are extremely numerous, and obviously very important, involving frequently large interests in valuable publications in which litigation to establish the rights of authors, publishers or infringers has been commenced or threatened. By the full records of copyright entries thus preserved, moreover, the Library of Congress (which is the property of the nation) has been enabled to secure what was before unattainable, namely, an approximately complete collection of all American books, etc., protected by copyright, since the legislation referred to went into effect. The system has been found in practice to give general satisfaction; the manner of securing copyright has been made plain and easy to all, the office of record being now a matter of public notoriety; and the test of experience during twenty years has established the system so thoroughly that none would be found to favor a return to the former methods. . . .

"The writers of America, with the steady and rapid growth of the art of making books, have come more and more to appreciate the value of their preservation, in complete and unbroken series, in the library of the government, the appropriate conservator of the nation's literature. Inclusive and not exclusive, as this library is wisely made by law, so far as copyright works are concerned, it preserves with impartial care the illustrious and the obscure. In its archives all sciences and all schools of opinion meet and mingle." [9]

The growth of the nation's cultural institutions in the last three decades of the century was striking. It was a period of expansion and reorganization of universities: The Johns Hopkins, Cornell, and other major schools were founded, and Harvard, Michigan, and Yale were given new life under new administrators and new programs.[10] American libraries purchased twenty-six important scholarly collections in Europe and brought them to America in this period.[11] The American Library Association was formed in 1876,[12] as was the American Chemical Society, to be followed in the eighties by more than a hundred learned societies in various disciplines.[13] The nineties saw revivals of interest in the arts and in fine printing; and new creative artists, composers, and writers were beginning to find a wide audience. Bibliography became a serious and dignified vocation as well as avocation; its devotees formed the Bibliographical Society of Chicago in 1899 and promoted its expansion into the Bibliographical Society of America in 1904.[14]

Interest in bibliographical activity had been steadily growing along both scholarly and commercial lines, among librarians and booksellers. The book trade became more effectively organized under Leypoldt and Bowker as the domestic production of books and periodicals increased; and comparable developments took place in the allied fields of music and art publishing.

Jewett's ideas regarding the desirability of centralizing bibliographic activities on a national basis, and his search for expeditious ways of performing them, were taken up and extended by many. In 1872 Henry Stevens anticipated modern mechanized techniques in proposing the use of the camera to contribute to the making of a definitive bibliographical record.[15] This suggestion for photographing title pages was discussed, though without practical effect, for many years to come[16] and was typical of the kind of imaginative attention bibliographical problems were receiving in these years.

In the eighties and nineties spokesmen for library and learned groups, especially in science, in both national and international gatherings, dreamed, talked, planned, and attempted to begin national and international bibliographical services. The drive for international cooperative ventures was especially strong in Europe, of course; American librarians followed these proposals closely,[17] though their own national bibliographical problems were of greater immediate concern.

In 1887, for example, during his service as librarian of the Minneapolis Athenaeum, Herbert Putnam advanced the hope that the largest library in each state or region would accept a responsibility to serve as a bibliographical center for its area, gathering together special collections of bibliographical tools and providing, free or at cost, bibliographical services to other libraries. Few other libraries were ready to act upon such a proposal; Melvil Dewey believed a better first objective would be the formation of *one* such bureau.[18]

This was the era of the library book-form catalog. The larger American libraries were devoting substantial sums to the publication of comprehensive catalogs of their collections; some of these, like that of the John Carter Brown collection (which was to go to Brown University in 1901), observed all of the bibliographical niceties and were presented in sumptuous editions.[19]

The *American Catalogue*, edited by Richard Rogers Bowker, was the standard current national bibliography of the period. As publisher of both *Publishers' Weekly* and the *Library Journal* he was an effective liaison officer serving both librarians and booksellers. His natural interest in bibliography prompted him to work toward the production of a complete American bibliography covering the nineteenth century, replacing not only Roorbach and Kelly but also his own *American Catalogue*. He advanced this proposal in March 1885,[20] urging librarians to cooperate with him by supplying entries for nineteenth-century American works in their collections. He referred to this proposal frequently in succeeding years.

Though Librarian of Congress Spofford shared with other leading bookmen this concern for the preservation of a national bibliographical record, his efforts to produce at least part of this record were not crowned with success—at least not on this basis. It required an additional motivation: the realization by Congress that its continued isolation from world-wide movements toward reciprocal copyright relationships was damaging rather than aiding the production of intellectual materials in the United States.

Agitation for an international copyright law had begun as early as 1837 with the consideration of a bill presented by Henry Clay. After 1870 new impetus was given to the movement by the interest of growing numbers of authors in the potentialities of foreign markets for their work, by the concern of American typographic industries for protection against foreign competition, and by those influential American publishers who were beginning to be aware of the harmful effects on the American book market of the low quality editions of British works with which the American pirates were flooding the market. Many international copyright bills were considered by Congress after 1870; while most of them failed, they served to kindle a growing flame of interest and belief in the ultimate desirability of such a measure. As Whitten and Fessler write: "The period from 1850 to 1890 can be characterized as one of almost sheer abandon on the part of publishers, although the movement for self-regulation steadily gained strength." [21]

Essentially, the act of 1891 extended the copyright statute to works by authors of foreign countries on certain conditions of reciprocal protection by the foreign country to works of United States authors. It had the salutary effect of enlarging the audiences of contemporary writers of both America and Europe, principally of the United States and Great Britain. While the total effect of the law was good, certain of its provisions created new problems for libraries and publishers.

One of these was that which prohibited the importation into the United States of any copyrighted book (and certain other materials) for which the type had been set or other production techniques had been performed outside of the United States. One exception to this provision was specified: persons purchasing such editions for use and not for sale could import, upon payment of duty, not more than two copies of any book at one time.

The publishers were not happy with this exception, as will be seen, because it enabled libraries and other institutions to acquire English editions of new works, often in preference to American editions readily available to them. The general revision of 1909 handled the problem in a complicated compromise provision with which few were satisfied: it continued to make it possible for libraries to acquire British editions, but reduced the number of copies which could be imported at any one time from two to one.

In its larger aspects, however, the 1891 law was a significant milestone in the cultural progress of the United States. Whitten and Fessler have stated that its importance "to the future of the publishing trade cannot be overemphasized as it effectively barred the practice of piracy and helped raise the standards of publishers." [22] Authors also benefited, as Lehmann-Haupt points out:

"The lack of legal protection for literary property had also very unfortunate effects upon the American authors. As long as it was possible to print the works of the most famous English writers and poets at ridiculously low costs, hardly a publisher in this country would consider encouraging unknown young American authors. Authorship as a profession, in fact, did not really become possible in America until after 1891, the date of the international copyright agreement. The comparatively indifferent standard of letters between 1860 and 1890 was surely not only due to cultural conditions. The best proof of the damaging effects of the bad conditions prevailing during most of the century was the appearance of vigorous new talent among American writers soon after the law of 1891 had been passed." [23]

The special significance of the 1891 law to this study, however, lies in the provisions authorizing publication of the *Catalog of Copyright Entries.* The circumstances under which they were produced merit detailed review.

FACTORS INFLUENCING THE FORM AND CONTENT OF THE CATALOGING PROVISIONS

Spofford not only believed the Act of July 8, 1870, had been a significant milestone in the history of both the Library of Congress and the development of the American copyright system; he evidently also believed it gave him authority to publish a catalog of the works copyrighted. Section 85 of the Act required the Librarian of Congress to "make an annual report to Congress of the number and *description* of copyright publications for which entries have been made during the year." [1] (Emphasis supplied.) The intent of this clause was explained in the presentation of the original bill [2] to the House of Representatives by Thomas A. Jenckes of Rhode Island, who stated that the bill provided "that the Librarian shall make a report every year to Congress of the number of those publications, and also a *catalogue of them.*" [3] (Emphasis supplied.) The House accepted the wording of the bill without discussion.

The Library's annual catalog had been keyed to a year calculated from December 1. Passage of the 1870 law persuaded the Librarian that it would be expedient henceforward to publish it as of January 1, since copyright deposits "are now accounted for by the calendar year." [4] While it might appear that by this simple change Spofford believed he was fulfilling his obligation to prepare a catalog of copyrighted works, it is clear that he did not equate the Library's catalog of accessions with such a catalog.

In the following year Spofford strongly urged the transfer of the registration of commercial prints and labels from the Library to the Patent Office, arguing: "Already the just public expectation, that a list of copyrights would be published periodically from the Office of the Librarian of Congress, has been unfulfilled and postponed in consequence of the manifest absurdity of filling such a record, which should represent the current product of American literature and science, with the titles of trifling labels and other 'prints' . . ." If the prints were removed from his charge he recommended: "that the Librarian be authorized and required to print a weekly list of copyright entries for public information, as the list of patents issued is now published in the Official Gazette of the Patent-Office, and that an appropriation of $1,600 for an additional assistant be authorized by law." [5]

The Act of June 18, 1874 [6] effected the desired transfer but did not clarify the Librarian's authority or duty to publish a catalog. As far as Spofford was concerned, however, he still felt under obligation to issue a list of copyright entries. In 1876 he called the attention of American librarians to the operations of the Act of 1870, adding that there were two objectives not yet attained: first, a new library building to house the great increase in accessions, and "secondly, the publication of a periodical list of copyright publications, either by original entry of titles or after actual appearance from the press. These objects it is hoped will ere long be accomplished." [7] The objective existed, but the means to accomplish it did not.

Achieving a separate library building had become the Librarian's major mission even before this. The growing copyright business was given priority attention on a day-to-day basis, not only as to the prompt handling of applications but also with respect to the preparation of an "index to copyright, by names of authors, publishers, and title, [which] must be kept constantly up-to-date. The extensive character of this business . . .

[adds] a conclusive argument . . . to the demonstration of the absolute necessity of erecting a separate building for the Library and copyright department conjoined." [8] To Spofford it was clear that when Congress enacted the 1870 law "it took a step which rendered the separation of this vast collection from the Capitol, sooner or later, a necessity." [9]

As time passed the incentive to issue a copyright catalog dwindled away. The problem of handling the rising tide of deposits in the eighties eventually affected the Library's ability to continue the preparation of its annual catalog of accessions. "The engrossing and rapidly increasing business of the copyright department . . . [absorbs] more and more the time of my assistants, while the cataloging and arrangement for prompt supply of all new additions to the Library . . . [and demands for service] leave no time for the preparation and printing of catalogues." [10] The last issue of the Library's author *Catalogue* appeared in 1880 and encompassed entries for less than one-fourth of the alphabet.

Spofford's interest in issuing "for public information" a catalog of copyright entries representing "the current product of American literature and science" does not appear to have been publicly expressed at any time during the intensive efforts beginning in 1885-86 which culminated in the Act of 1891. The proposals for a catalog were instead expressly pointed to serve the purpose of preventing the importation into the United States of pirated editions infringing works under copyright in the United States.

The first legislative proposal made to Congress clearly providing for the publication of lists of copyright entries was contained in Senate bill number 1178, introduced on January 21, 1886, by Senator Jonathan Chace of Rhode Island. It was this bill "which was finally enacted as the so-called 'International Copyright Law' of March 3, 1891," [11] not, however, without change. The bill as a whole was the subject of extensive argument both in committee and in Congress. Debate involved principally those sections providing for the extension of the copyright privilege to noncitizens and nonresidents, the limitation of protection of the works of such authors by the requirement that they be manufactured in the United States, and the restriction of importation of foreign editions of works under copyright in the United States. The catalog provision was tied directly to the importation provision.

Summarized, the catalog provision of the Chace Bill of 1886 provided: lists of articles registered by deposit of title or description were to be published weekly or more frequently for the use of collectors of customs and postmasters handling foreign mails; these lists were to be published by the Secretary of the Treasury from information supplied by the Librarian of Congress; the lists were also to be made available to anyone desiring them for not more than $5 per year; receipts of recording fees for works registered by noncitizens and nonresidents (which were double those for citizens and residents) were to be used expressly to defray the printing costs of the lists; the Librarian was to receive an additional $1,000 a year in compensation for the added responsibility of compiling the data to be printed; and the Secretary of the Treasury and the Postmaster General were empowered to make regulations necessary to prevent the importation of the prohibited works.

In the five years ensuing between the introduction of the Chace Bill and the enactment of the Act of March 3, 1891, a number of changes took place. As passed, the act provided that the lists were to contain only those works wherein the copyright had been completed by the deposit of copies in conformity with the manufacturing provision; the provision for an increase in the Librarian's salary was dropped out; the rules and regulations of the Secretary of the Treasury and the Postmaster General were required to be so made and enforced as to admit into the United States those works specifically exempted from the prohibition-of-importation clause. These changes stemmed largely from a tightening of the manufacturing provision, resulting from the strong positions taken by the typographic and lithographic unions, and from the compromises effected when the prohibition-of-importation clause ran into the strong opposition of certain senators during the final days of debate in February 1891.

The likelihood that such opposition would develop was anticipated in the 1886 hearings on the Chace Bill, notably by Henry C. Lea, the Philadelphia publisher, who predicted, "The prohibition of importation will naturally be objected to by a few gentlemen who collect handsome libraries." [12] In spite of such far-sightedness, the publishers entirely underestimated the strength of the opposition that was to develop.

The 1886 hearings were marked by spirited protests by representatives of pirating publishers who seized upon the provision providing for the publication of lists for the assistance of customs officers as an opening through which to attack the entire bill. They castigated the bill for setting up "machinery of the Government" to "work as detectives and informers." [13] Lea's declaration that it had been "the absence of any arrangement for keeping the customs officers advised of what books are copyrighted" that had made past efforts to stop the entry of piratical editions "virtually ineffective" [14] was treated with some derision. "Our vast civilization suddenly discovers that the foreign copyright is so much more difficult of enforcement that we must set this machinery at work." [15] The catalog provision came up for discussion simply because it was the "machinery" devised to prevent unauthorized importation: the point really at issue was the importation of British editions.

It is likely that the cataloging provision was drafted at the instigation of the book publishers. George Haven Putnam ascribed authorship of the first draft submitted to Senator Chace to "the authors and the publishers," [16] probably the American Copyright League, of which he was secretary and prime mover. When further changes in the bill were made to meet the insistence of the typographical unions that typesetting in the United States be made a condition of American manufacture, and the importation of all foreign editions of works copyrighted in the United States be prohibited, these changes were prepared by Lea.[17] Thorvald Solberg, eight years before becoming the first Register of Copyrights, drafted a bill which was introduced by Senator Orville Hitchcock Platt of Connecticut on December 4, 1889. The phraseology of Solberg's draft of the cataloging provision was almost identical with that of the act as passed.

Final action on international copyright legislation began on December 1, 1890, with a call by President Benjamin Harrison in his message to Congress, reiterating earlier pleas for favorable consideration of the bill. In the debates in the House of Representatives on the following two days no mention was made of the provision for publishing catalogs. In spite of the stalling tactics of opponents (principally from the Midwest) the bill's manager, Representative William Edgar Simonds of Connecticut, secured favorable action on December 3.[18]

In the Senate the bill's sponsor, Senator Platt, endeavored to shepherd the bill through on February 9, 1891, without extensive debate and without amendment. Senator Eugene Hale of Maine protested these tactics strongly: "no set of men have any right to arrogate to themselves the wisdoms that shall contain all propositions which shall be carried into this bill . . ."[19] This objection spurred other controversy resulting notably in an amendment introduced and eloquently advocated by Senator John Sherman of Ohio, former Secretary of the Treasury, and Chairman of the Joint Committee on the Library between 1881 and 1884. The effect of his amendment would have been to permit unrestricted importation of works manufactured abroad, subject only to the payment of importation duties.[20] Senator Platt, undoubtedly agonized at the thought of the months and years of compromise that would have been wasted if the amendment were passed, spoke strongly against it: "The fundamental idea of a copyright is the exclusive right to vend . . . It is the right to vend within the country where the copyright is granted that gives value to the work of the author."[21] Nevertheless, the Sherman amendment was accepted.[22]

The death of his brother, William Tecumseh Sherman, on February 14, necessitated John Sherman's absence from the Senate for several days. In that time and after further discussion, the copyright bill was remanded to a joint conference committee to reconcile the opposing viewpoints of those favoring prohibition of importation of foreign editions and those arguing for permissive importation. After much discussion, agreement was finally reached on March 3, 1891,[23] in the late hours of the night. Sherman's amendment to permit unrestricted importation subject to payment of duty was lost, in spite of his continued fight for it on returning to the Senate; however, the original language prohibiting importation was also lost. The compromise provision accepted by the conference committee permitted the importation of only limited numbers of copies of foreign editions, and then under rather involved conditions. In all of the discussions the question of publishing a catalog was not raised, although it was clear that the purpose of such a catalog was to assist those required to enforce the nonimportation provision.

George Haven Putnam bitterly assailed the "eleventh-hour experts of the Senate or the House, men who, having looked into the matter over night, feel assured that they know all about it. The action of the Senate in February, 1891 . . . is a fair example of the kind of amateur and haphazard legislation referred to."[24] Fourteen years later the memory of the events of March 3, 1891, was still fresh in the minds of many of the conferees working with Herbert Putnam and Thorvald Solberg in 1905 and 1906 on a new general revision. Robert Underwood Johnson of the American Copyright League said that, up to the night of March third "it was confidently expected that the text of the bill would contain a . . . mandatory non-importation clause. . . . At half-past seven o'clock on that evening . . . I was informed . . . that the Conference Committee . . . had decided that the mandatory clause should be stricken out, and the permissive clause should be inserted." The typographical unions felt themselves betrayed. The proponents of the bill felt sure that neither of the sponsors (Senator Platt and Representative Simonds) was responsible but that "the other members . . . [of the joint conference committee] had insisted upon [the permissive] clause in the interest . . . of libraries and educational interests of the general public." [25]

The bill as finally passed on March 3, 1891, contained substantially the same provisions regarding the production of weekly lists as were contained in S. 1178 of 1886 (the Chace Bill) but in a different arrangement. The complete wording is as follows:

"Sec. 4. That section forty-nine hundred and fifty-eight of the Revised Statutes be, and the same is hereby, amended so that it will read as follows:

"'Sec. 4958. The Librarian of Congress shall receive from the persons to whom the services designated are rendered the following fees:

"'First. For recording the title or description of any copyright book or other article, fifty cents.

"'Second. For every copy under seal of such record actually given to the person claiming the copyright, or his assigns, fifty cents.

"'Third. For recording and certifying any instrument of writing for the assignment of a copyright, one dollar.

"'Fourth. For every copy of an assignment, one dollar.

"'All fees so received shall be paid into the Treasury of the United States: *Provided,* That the charge for recording the title or description of any article entered for copyright, the production of a person not a citizen or resident of the United States, shall be one dollar, to be paid as above into the Treasury of the United States, to defray the expenses of lists of copyrighted articles as hereinafter provided for.

"'And it is hereby made the duty of the Librarian of Congress to furnish to the Secretary of the Treasury copies of the entries of titles of all books and other articles wherein the copyright has been completed by the deposit of two copies of such book printed from type set within the limits of the United States, in accordance with the provisions of this act and by the deposit of two copies of such other article made or produced in the United States; and the Secretary of the Treasury is hereby directed to prepare and print, at intervals of not more than a week, catalogues of such title-entries for distribution to the collectors of customs of the United States and to the postmasters of all post-offices receiving foreign mails, and such weekly lists, as they are issued, shall be furnished to all parties desiring them, at a sum not exceeding five dollars per annum; and the Secretary and the Postmaster-General are hereby empowered and required to make and enforce such rules and regulations as shall prevent the importation into the United States except upon the conditions above specified of all articles prohibited by this act.' "[26]

Authorization for the publication of the copyright record by the Government was finally in being. The recording fees to be paid by those who were not citizens or residents of the United States were to be used to defray the expenses involved in issuing the catalogs. No other objective of the weekly lists was specified in the law other than that of preventing the importation of piratical works from abroad.

4 The *Catalog of Copyright Entries*, 1891-1909

DESCRIPTION

The weekly list authorized by the Act of 1891 duly appeared. The first number was a nine-page pamphlet issued under the title *Catalogue of Title-Entries of Books and Other Articles.*[1] Arrangement was by format or "subject matter" headings. In these early issues a profusion of such format headings was employed; those commonly used included books, periodicals, musical compositions, dramatic compositions, lithographs, engravings, chromos, charts, drawings, and maps.

Under these general headings the individual entries were recorded in two columns: Books [etc.] and Proprietors. The first column included a brief title of the work, edition or volume, and the author's name in brief form; the second column gave the proprietor's name, and the city and state of his residence. The arrangement of entries under the format headings may have been the order of recordation following receipt of deposit copies and fee. To the present user's eye the order is completely haphazard.

The first of a long series of changes in the *Catalog* is evident in issue number 20 (that for November 16-21, 1891); the periodicals entered in this issue were arranged alphabetically by their titles. The obvious advantages of the arrangement were not extended to any of the other format groups until 1895. In the issue for July 22-27, 1895 (No. 212), musical compositions were arranged alphabetically by proprietor for the first time. This pattern was adopted for books in the issue for November 11-16 (No. 228) and for all other groups by the end of the year. Periodicals continued to be listed alphabetically by title.

The belated adoption of this most elementary system of arrangement is difficult to explain in the light of the purpose the lists were presumed to serve: that of enabling customs officers and postmasters to prevent the importation of piratical copies. Each issue would have had to be scanned completely on receipt and the titles of works stored away in the memory of each officer; searching in them would clearly have been a hopeless operation. Possibly the joint responsibility for publication—that of the Library of Congress for the preparation of copy and that of the Treasury Department for printing—was a fundamental factor underlying this weakness of the early issues. Spofford's complaint of 1892 regarding the additional labor involved in preparation of the *Catalog*[2] suggests that he felt it impossible to devote the time needed to correct its faults.

The completion of the new Library building, the creation of the Copyright Office, and the appointment of John Russell Young as Librarian and of Thorvald Solberg as first Register of Copyrights, all in 1897, opened a new era for the *Catalog*. Until this time the weekly issues had been numbered consecutively from 1 through 339. The latter number covered the final week of calendar 1897 and ran to 112 pages. Beginning with music in August, Solberg had, by the end of 1897, reorganized the *Catalog* by arranging all entries, still in their format groupings, alphabetically by title and by including in each issue a combined proprietor index to all materials.

It was in 1897 also that the published catalog for the first time contained the date of receipt of deposit copies (issue No. 324, September 13-18). It is interesting to recall that this had been a characteristic feature of all the entries prepared by William Elliot for 1796 through May 1825, and of the later entries prepared by Charles Coffin Jewett in 1849 and 1850. Beginning in 1898 the date of copyright and the registration number were added to the entry. The *Catalog of Copyright Entries* at last became more than a simple record; it was a search tool which was arranged to make information accessible regarding all works whose registration had been completed by the deposit of copies. This it has continued to be to the present day. While the pre-1898 issues cannot now be effectively searched, the *Catalog* has consistently remained, through its entire existence, a published record of all works for which copyright registration had been completed by the deposit of copies, and, after 1909, of those for which registration had been renewed for a second term. In sixty-seven years it has recorded more than 9,500,000 monographs and serial issues in a wide variety of forms, including renewal registrations.

With the 1898 issues, the *Catalog* acquired volume numbering. Each volume now consisted of the weekly issues of three months.

When Spofford had been given responsibility for the copyright system in 1870 he at once began preparation of an index on cards which, while not required by the law, provided access to specific recordations of registrations of title in the Record Books. Until 1898 this remained strictly an index; to secure complete information about any work, or about its registration, it was necessary to consult the Record Books as well as the card index. The published catalog had relatively little relationship to this card file at this time: it was limited to those works for which registration had been completed by the deposit of copies; it contained more information about each work than the card index, but less than the Record Books.

The Librarian's report for 1897 announced: "A new method of indexing has been arranged by which the index cards are made for the titles on the day of their receipt." [3] These were more than index cards, however, for each contained, in addition to proprietor, author, title, and edition statement, the classification symbol, registration number, date of registration, and date of receipt of deposit copies. For every work registered a card was filed under the name of the copyright proprietor. Additional cards containing complete information were filed under author and/or title, and under area for maps. "These index cards . . . become part of the permanent indexes of the copyright office, and are also used as the copy for the 'Catalogue of title-entries' . . ."[4] From this time forward the published catalogs substantially duplicated the information contained in the card files respecting original registrations completed by the deposit of copies, and renewal registrations.

In the quarterly volume (Vol. *26*) of the *Catalog* for January-March 1901 a combined quarterly index was provided which included index entries for all proprietors, for the authors of dramas and books proper, and for the titles of periodicals, dramas, and anonymous works. In the next volume, April-June 1901, the index was enlarged to include the subject words in the titles of maps.

These improvements in both the card files and the published catalog were in recognition of the need to provide to searchers more than one heading through which the information desired could be located. At the same time the Register was reluctant to extend these facilities to the point where they would encourage uses of the record for other than copyright purposes: "No attempt is made to index the titles as such; that is to say, in order to show that any given title has been used. So long as the copyright law does not secure the use of a registered title to some one person to the exclusion of all others, there would seem to be no justification in adding to the already large index upward of 100,000 cards annually simply to show that certain forms of words have been used by one or more persons as designations for books, maps, music, photographs, etc., registered for copyright protection."[5] This kind of thinking has probably served to restrict and limit the utility of the copyright record through the years much more than any deficiencies to be found in the record itself.

The *Catalog* was further improved in a number of respects during the next several years. It will serve no useful purpose to recount these in detail, although changes of consequence will be noted whenever appropriate. At this point it is desirable to assess, insofar as that is possible, the kind of public attention the *Catalog* was receiving in the years preceding the passage of the present copyright law.

FACTORS INFLUENCING DEVELOPMENT

There is no suggestion to be found in the hearings or debates leading to the passage of the Act of 1891 that the *Catalog of Copyright Entries* was being authorized for any other purpose than to prevent importation of piratical editions. Considering that it was the group of book publishers, primarily, who conceived and expounded the need for a weekly catalog to serve this purpose, it is somewhat surprising to find their principal representative, Richard Rogers Bowker, advocating another use for it within four months after the law went into effect. This proposal was aired on October 16, 1891, during the San Francisco Conference of the American Library Association, in a series of resolutions introduced by Mr. Bowker:

"The Association took some action relating to the passage of the Copyright act. One of the questions of the Copyright bill was the provision of a weekly list of copyrighted books, which has been since sent to the Treasury Department in a more [or less?] roundabout way since the 1st of July. It may be worth while to call the attention of this conference to the fact that this list contains the name of every book and pamphlet copyrighted in this country. It is, therefore, a most thorough foundation for a national bibliography, and I have had some talk with Mr. Spofford as to the desirability of making this a bibliographical record:—

"*Resolved,* That the A.L.A. records its gratification at the passage of an international copyright act, as promoting justice to authors of books and the development of American literature.

"*Resolved,* That the Association suggests to the librarian of Congress, that in the weekly list of copyright deposits full bibliographical data of books and pamphlets (except those solely commercial) be given, as the best possible basis for an adequate national bibliography.

"*Resolved,* That, in case of the amendment of the act, the Association suggests that the publication of the weekly list be transferred to the jurisdiction of the librarian of Congress, and that he be authorized to receive subscriptions for, or to provide for, the distribution of the list." [1]

Bowker was also, at this time, actively trying to find the means of producing a comprehensive bibliography of nineteenth-century United States publications. In the preface of his *American Catalogue* for 1884-90 he acknowledged the passage of the Act of 1891 in terms of much satisfaction: "This will be a great benefit, not only to American literature and to the American book trade, but to American bibliography in particular, as the new law requires the deposit of all copyright books, simultaneously with their publication, as an essential condition of copyright. It is therefore to be presumed that all books of any importance published in America will be recorded in the Library of Congress and thus an official basis will be possible for American bibliography." [2]

The appearance of a printed catalog based on copyright deposits attracted early attention in England. Henry R. Tedder, in a paper presented on April 17, 1893, before the Bibliographical Society,[3] believed it possible for an official current record to be produced for British works, although he acknowledged that copyright in Great Britain had never been intended, either by publishers or lawyers, as an official record of current literature.[4] Describing procedures that might be employed, he enlarged upon the proposal made many years before by Henry Stevens.[5] The bibliography could be accomplished, "if each copy of a book when published had to bear attached to it a printed slip containing the following particulars: (1) A reduced photograph of the title page. (2) The same set out in type. (3) A collation. (4) Perhaps a few words of explanation whenever a fanciful title made this necessary, or any other information which may be considered desirable. . . . Two copies of this slip would be handed in on registration; one copy might be stamped in some way and returned as a voucher, and the other preserved for registration. A full description of every book would thus be preserved for all time. Catalogues prepared from these slips, with all necessary editorial prunings, could be issued by the Register in weekly, monthly, or annual instalments, with necessary indexes of authors, titles, subjects, and publishers. . . . Catalogue slips in less elaborate shapes have been already printed by some English and American publishers, and by the Smithsonian Institution." [6]

The *Catalog* stimulated the imaginations of others in the United States[7] such as that of G. W. Cole. The library world was at the threshold of a golden era: it was far better to include too much ephemera in such a listing than too little, "provided, of course," wrote Cole, "that the matter recorded is somewhere preserved in a manner that it can be referred to by those who may hereafter become interested in it." [8]

The American Library Association in December 1895 heard a proposal that the number of copyright deposit copies to be required of publishers be increased to seven, so that regional libraries in Chicago, New Orleans, Denver, and San Francisco might receive them in addition to the Library of Congress, and that state libraries might receive one copy of each work by an author resident of that state.[9] This proposal was referred to the committee on public documents, where it at first received relatively little attention in view of that committee's deep engagement in following developments for the distribution of United States government documents under the new law passed in January 1895. Bowker welcomed the bibliographical work of the new Superintendent of Documents, since it would relieve him of having to try to cover United States documents in forthcoming issues of the *American Catalogue*.[10]

Encouraged by the bibliographical interest he found everywhere, Mr. Bowker announced in 1895 that work had already begun on a bibliography of the nineteenth-century American books published to 1876 which were not listed in the 1876 issue of the *American Catalogue*.[11]

Herbert Putnam, then librarian of the Boston Public Library, was one of the group of librarians invited to appear, late in 1896, at hearings before the Joint Committee on the Library to offer suggestions and counsel to the committee regarding the condition of the Library and its future. All of these librarians spoke forcefully on the desirability of the Library's taking leadership in the performance of national bibliographical services of various kinds. In a letter to the committee dated December 7, 1896, Putnam became rather more specific than the others and outlined in some detail the values, to the Library and to the nation's libraries, of printing catalog entries on cards and making them generally available by purchase. "[It] is to be hoped the National Library will be able to catalogue once and for all the new publications under the copyright law, to print these catalogue entries upon cards, and to furnish duplicates of these cards (for some proper charge) to other American libraries . . ." [12] Putnam thus not only anticipated the Library's printed-card program, soon to be inaugurated, but gave expression to the generally held concept that the program would inevitably depend upon the operation of the copyright deposit system.

Thorvald Solberg was shortly to express, four months before receiving his appointment as first Register of Copyrights, a plan for achieving an international bibliography on a scale no one else seems ever to have contemplated. While the concept he advanced was remarkable for its scope it came clearly and naturally from the well of his own experience.[13] By the time he was twenty-two years of age he had compiled an index to the "Annual Book Trade Catalogue" [14] (undoubtedly the *Publishers' Trade List Annual,* the first issue of which had appeared in 1873). Though his index evidently was never published, it anticipated a need satisfied briefly by the Leypoldt indexes of 1902-04, and currently by the Bowker Company's *Books in Print.* He had also attended his first book trade convention at Put-in Bay, Ohio, in July 1874. At that time he demonstrated his interest in bibliography by addressing to the editor of *Publishers' Weekly* a courteous but forthright expression of dissatisfaction:

"If there was anything with which I was not fully contented, it was only that the Convention gave expression to so little interest in the subject of bibliography. To be sure, they made your valuable journal the official organ of the Association, and accepted Mr. Steiger's offer of preparing classified catalogues.

But the former we looked upon being done as a matter of course, and had not contemplated the possibility of its being neglected, and the reception of Mr. Steiger's offer was but a very cool and matter-of-fact acceptance of a most generous proposal.

"I looked forward to some one advancing resolutions in support of the 'Finding List,' or some other practical bibliography; but as no one else seemed to think of the matter, I prepared a few resolutions to the effect, that a committee be appointed to consider and report on the bibliographical wants of the trade and the best means of alleviating them. But as I only prepared them during Thursday's session under the mistaken impression that there was an afternoon session that day, the rush of so much other business crowded them out entirely and so I reluctantly saw the Convention close without anything of importance having been moved in a matter that interests us so much, or even a vote of thanks having been given to those who have expended time and labor in improving the bibliography we now have." [15]

Solberg had then been in the book business for five years. Two years later he joined the staff of the Library of Congress. During this period, 1876 to 1889, he engaged in the first of several bibliographical undertakings in fields of his special interests, notably Scandinavian literature,[16] and copyright. His extensive *Bibliography of Literary Property,* completed in 1885, was published as an appendix to Bowker's *Publishers' Weekly* articles on the copyright law,[17] when they were issued in book form at the beginning of the final successful drive for an international law.

In 1889 he joined the staff of the Boston Book Company and in the next three years made a number of trips to Europe to acquire books and journals for his company, in response to orders from American libraries. A physical breakdown interrupted his career between 1893 and 1896.[18] In the latter year he returned to his company, and within a few months persuaded his employer to begin publishing the *Bulletin of Bibliography,* which he had originally proposed about 1890.[19] His chief assistant in 1896 was Frederick W. Faxon,[20] later to take over the company and give it his name.

It was at this time, March 11, 1897, that he addressed a meeting of the New York Library Club and advanced his proposal for an international bibliography. A contemporary report condensed his remarks as follows:

"The present time, he said, demands not only a prompter and more complete record of book production, but a more exact and elaborate record. This need is not only current but retroactive, and one of the sure claims upon the coming century is, not only that it shall produce its complete weekly, monthly, or yearly catalog, but that it shall go back and recatalog the world's books according to the new methods. The need for these two things, a regular periodic publication of all titles of all current books and great national bibliographies, adequately cataloging all published books, is becoming greater daily. The great improvement in bibliographical machinery makes this vast project practicable and the establishment of the International Copyright Union renders its accomplishment possible.

"[A beginning in this direction had already been made through the Bureau's monthly journal *Le Droit d'Auteur* in] a series of elaborate annual summaries of the book production of the countries for which figures were available. The incompleteness of this record [and its lack of uniformity led to the suggestion that all copyrighted works in Berne Union countries be registered at the Bureau to provide a basis not only for the compilation of uniform statistics but also for] a catalog of these works by author and title. This latter broadened into a proposal to carry such a catalog back to the date of the Berne Treaty, December 5, 1887, by compilations by each country of all copyright literature produced since that date. From this point it was but a single leap to a conception of a universal catalog of books going back to the very origin of printing." [21]

The basing of a national bibliography upon the copyright system was a widely held ideal. Mr. Putnam shared it in 1896, while still at Boston, as indicated by his writing to the Joint

Committee on the Library that one of the undertakings appropriate to the Library would be the production of "a catalogue of all books received under the copyright law." [22]

Mr. Bowker felt free to suggest to an international meeting of librarians in London, July 16, 1897, his concept of the close relationship that should exist between the copyright record, national bibliography, and the printed-card program: "Our national library, still called the Library of Congress, has not yet taken its proper place, filled in large measure in the mother-country by the British Museum, of heading and centralizing bibliographical work. The few printed volumes of its catalog are partial, incomplete, and antiquated, and the physical congestion prevailing until lately has made progress difficult. The *Weekly Register* of copyrights also has not been bibliographically useful. But the national library is now removing its books to the finest library building in the country, and it is in the process of reorganization, the registry of copyrights being made a distinctive department. This gives the library a remarkable opportunity. For a fee of 50 cents, additional to a like fee for copyright entry, the Register of Copyrights is obliged to return a record of copyright, and it is the practice of copyright proprietors to pay the double fee and obtain the record in all cases. If, in the new developments, it should be arranged that this record shall take the shape of a printed card for catalog entry, and if duplicates of such cards could be supplied to subscribing libraries, a great step forward in practical bibliography would be made." [23]

The same concept was endorsed by the 1900 conference in Paris of the Institut Internationale de Bibliographie (Brussels), which urged the enactment of improved copyright laws in the various countries as a contribution to the international organization of national bibliography.[24]

Actually, the Library had already taken steps to prepare for the eventual distribution of cards; according to J. C. M. Hanson the Library's Catalogue Division took over the task of preparing copy for the "books proper" section of the weekly copyright catalog on May 1, 1898: "[This action] opened the way for the manifolding of entries on printed cards for all books added through operation of the copyright law, about one-fourth of the total accessions, and resulted in the opening of the first card catalogue for the public and, what was of prime importance to the staff, an official catalogue located in the catalogue room. Fifty copies of each entry were printed on standard-size cards of medium weight. Besides a second copy of the dictionary catalogue for the staff, it was decided to prepare also a third copy ultimately to be placed in the Capitol." [25]

A bare suggestion of the changes in process was made public in 1897: "A weekly bulletin of publications received at the Library, under the provisions of the copyright law, is furnished to the Treasury by the Librarian and printed for the use of the collectors of customs at ports of entry to aid in the suppression of copyright publications printed abroad without permission of the proprietor. This bulletin has been carefully rearranged with new bibliographical features, giving it a special value as a catalogue of current American literature. Numbers of the edition are taken by subscribers at the cost of $5 a year, payable at any United States custom-house." [26]

The report for the following year gives fuller expression to the plans of the Library, and suggests that for the first time the *Catalog of Copyright Entries* was seriously thought of as a contribution to current national bibliography.

"By the amendment of the copyright law of 1891 Congress made it the duty of the Librarian of Congress to prepare a weekly catalogue of all books and other articles for which copyright had been granted. This publication was designed, primarily, to serve the collectors of customs in the prevention of the illegal importation of copyright works. To render it more useful for this purpose and give it special bibliographical value the articles catalogued have been classified, and each issue provided with a complete index of copyright proprietors. The work is edited and arranged so as to comply strictly with the law, which requires that it should contain a complete transcript of the title entry, and that each title should state the name of the copyright proprietor, the date and number of the copyright entry and the date of the receipt of the copies deposited to complete the copyright.

"This publication is of special importance as the official contemporaneous record of the growth of American literature and American art. Its value in this particular is not only current, but permanent; as a historical record of the first production of the books and other articles recorded, its usefulness to the student will increase with time. Every effort has been made to improve it as a chronicle of current literature. The titles are prepared with completeness and arranged for ready reference. Care is taken also to number each title so that statistics can be obtained of the annual intellectual and artistic progress of the nation. Some idea of the volume of this productiveness is conveyed by the mere statement that this Catalogue of Title Entries for a single year requires four octavo volumes of 1,000 pages each." [27]

The Library's use of the improved bibliographical entries was explained: "Beginning with May 14, 1898, the catalogue department undertook . . . to prepare the entries for books proper in the catalogue of title entries. This made it possible to cut up and mount on cards copies of the weekly catalogue, giving a second copy of the official catalogue for copyright books after that date." [28] The setting up of a printing office in the Library to print cards for other than copyright accessions was also proposed in this report.[29]

During this time the documents committee of the American Library Association supported an amendment to the appropriations bill introduced December 18, 1897, which would have transferred the office of Superintendent of Documents to the Library of Congress. The committee believed that that portion of the Superintendent's work dealing with the collection and cataloging of public documents properly belonged there.[30] The amendment however failed of passage. In the same report (August 1898) the committee reviewed the proposal of Samuel H. Ranck regarding the creation of additional copyright depositories, the reception it had received in the public press, and certain alternative suggestions that had been made. After corresponding with the Copyright Office, and learning of its practice of retaining one copy in the Copyright Office "in special record deposit," the committee found itself, in view of all the considerations involved, unable to recommend favorable action on Mr. Ranck's plan.[31]

Nevertheless, the prospect of improved bibliographical services emerging from an improved copyright system continued to hold its attractiveness.

"Bibliographical work," wrote W. S. Merrill, "is rarely undertaken by governmental direction, and then mostly in monarchical countries, while the work is actually done at some large depository of new publications. Germany is an instance of private enterprise producing a trade catalogue which ranks as a bibliography. England has no official register of new works, and it is only recently that the bulletin of our own Register of Copyrights has assumed bibliographical form at all.

"Were a bibliographical bureau, equipped with expert bibliographers, established in every country in connection with the central depository of newly copyrighted works, we should have at once, in the publications of these bureaus taken collectively, a nearly exhaustive universal bibliography of current publications; while taken individually these records would be national bibliographies of the first importance. It is to be hoped that the present tendency in our Copyright Office will result in preparing the title entries for all works copyrighted by the Library of Congress in truly bibliographical shape, and thus, in following the example of Italy, further the advance toward the unification of all national bibliography." [32]

The librarian of the John Crerar Library of Chicago, Aksel G. S. Josephson, advocated the creation of a National Bibliographical Commission to be supported and subsidized by scientific and professional societies, institutions, and libraries. He brought this plan to the attention of the American Library Association, the American Historical Association, and the Bibliographical Society during 1900-01.[33] In 1902 he illuminated his proposal with details; the bibliographical institute to be set up would produce "a complete American bibliography":

"The entries [would be prepared] in co-operation by a number of leading libraries, the field of work to be divided according to the particular strength of each co-operating library. For instance, the literature previous to 1700 might be recorded by the New York Public Library; the copyrighted books after 1870 by the Library of Congress; the literature of medicine by the Surgeon General's Library; that of geology by the United States Geological Survey, etc. . . .

"It would naturally be divided in two parts, the bibliography of current literature and the retrospective bibliography of the past. . . ." [34]

Mr. Spofford by this time exhibited some disillusionment: "Notwithstanding the hopeless nature of the quest, it is true that some men of learning have essayed what have been termed universal bibliographies." [35] He did not really commit himself on the possibility of making the *Catalog of Copyright Entries* a national bibliography, but did suggest—the first time anyone had done so—that it might not be serving the purposes for which it had been authorized in 1891: the interception of imported piratical editions.[36]

Mr. Bowker had found the weekly copyright lists useful in the preparation of the 1895-1900 issue of the *American Catalogue,* particularly with respect to books which had not been received in the offices of *Publishers' Weekly.*[37] Even before the Library began distributing its cards, therefore, the *Catalog of Copyright Entries* was making a definite, practical contribution to American trade bibliography.

Herbert Putnam became Librarian of Congress on April 5, 1899;[38] he launched the distribution of printed Library of Congress cards in the summer and fall of 1901.[39] Preparatory work had begun as early as May 1, 1898, as we have seen, with cards printed from the type composed for the *Catalog of Copyright Entries* being run off in sets of fifty. Beginning in December 1900, after a branch of the Government Printing Office had been set up in the Library,[40] the number of cards printed per title was increased in anticipation of card orders.

Operation of the card program in the early years, C. H.

Hastings recalls, revealed some points of conflict between the Library and the Copyright Office:

"The orders for cards soon demonstrated that a considerable percentage of books with copyright claims in them were being deposited late or not at all. When the Copyright Office was asked to get them in, it was disposed to take the view that questions as to deposit or non-deposit of copies was the business of the Copyright Office exclusively. . . . The Card Division strongly urged that the American edition be purchased [when not received by copyright], whereas the established practice was to purchase the English edition. The Card Division also desired to have non-copyrighted books purchased on the strength of orders received for cards, instead of waiting for them to be ordered for the reading-room service, or on the recommendations of the chiefs of divisions. The Chief of the Accessions Division, Superintendent of the Reading Room, and other officials maintained that the Library would be flooded with popular books and suffer serious financial loss if the change [i.e. to purchase of American editions] was made.

"The cards for copyrighted books thus far printed had been decked out with copyright numbers, dates, and symbols, and the Catalogue Division had added a few symbols of its own. The subscribers objected to such extraneous matter and the Card Division urged that it be taken off.

"The struggle over the above-mentioned objectives was severe during the first two years and continued intermittently for several years. The weapons were chiefly memoranda to the Librarian, and scores of them were written, some of them quite voluminous. . . ." [41]

All of the routines required for the handling of deposits—examining and cataloging in the Copyright Office and selection, cataloging, and forwarding to the collections by the Library, in addition to card distribution—have, in fact, been a cause of recurring difficulty between copyright office and library personnel since the Copyright Office was created in 1897. This was not a one-sided matter; in 1908, for example, F. W. Ashley, the Chief of the Correspondence Division of the Copyright

Office put it plainly in a memorandum to the Register: "The work done by the Copyright Office is rendered more complex and difficult by reason of the connection of the Office with the Library of Congress. Were the Office an independent bureau, its duties would be confined to receiving and recording titles, receiving, crediting and filing such copies as come to hand, indexing entries, recording assignments, furnishing copies of the records, and answering inquiries. But its relation to the Library of Congress necessitates the performance of a considerable service beyond the normal functions of a record office, and requiries [sic] also that the Office processes be coordinated with those of other divisions of the Library. This extra service consumes considerable time and labor, and renders necessary the employment of a larger force of clerks than would otherwise be required." [42]

The bibliographical services of the Library of Congress were expanding meanwhile under Herbert Putnam's direction, with the support and encouragement of leading American librarians. The distribution of Library of Congress cards was having great impact upon librarians and bibliographers. Putnam's crystallization of the Library's service objectives was to have a permanent effect upon its activities, which were to include a substantial bibliographical publishing program and the institution of an interlibrary loan service. The relationship of copyright to these activities was known to library leaders, at least: a state librarian urged increasing the number of deposit copies to three so that state libraries might build up comprehensive collections of the works of authors residing in the respective states; a university librarian pointed out that Mr. Putnam's program was simply the carrying out of an obligation which the Library took upon itself in becoming the copyright depository; a public librarian urged the reconstruction of the nineteenth-century copyright record by instituting a program for collecting early copyright books back to 1790; a special librarian thought the Library should eventually print a catalog of its American works.[43] Finally, the printed-card program elicited the enthusiastic interest of some Englishmen, one of whom called for international cooperation in the production of printed cards for works in other languages.[44]

The American Library Association issued in 1902 the first edition of the standard American guide to reference books. The *Catalog of Copyright Entries* was duly recorded, and was placed, together with *Publishers' Weekly*, under the heading: Bibliography—National and Trade—American—Weekly. The entry for the *Catalog*, covering all issues to 1902, included the following annotation: "Weekly. The most complete record of current American publications, including books, periodicals, music, engravings, etc. No prices." [45]

The Register of Copyrights tentatively suggested undertaking a retrospective indexing operation of some magnitude: "It is very desirable that all copyright registrations should be thoroughly indexed in order that the frequent inquiries received at the office relative to entries made, or supposed to have been made, can be fully and authoritatively answered. The current indexing is fairly complete, the index cards for the fiscal year numbering nearly 140,000, and this thorough indexing dates back to January 1, 1898. Entries from 1870 to 1897, however, numbering nearly one million, are not so adequately indexed, and it is a constant occurrence to receive inquiries as to entries made during this period, which can not be authoritatively answered, because these entries are at present incompletely indexed. The still earlier entries, from 1790 to 1870, in the record books of the offices of the clerks of the district courts, have no general index, but only imperfect indexes for each volume. It would be a decided gain to the clients of the Copyright Office if all the entries made from 1790 to 1897, inclusive, could be indexed in the same complete and careful manner in which the entries made since the latter date have been indexed, and I trust Congress will be willing to grant a sufficient force to enable the undertaking of this work." [46] So far as is known this proposal was not repeated at that time, although the desirability of making the full record useful has been advanced in more recent days by Roberts and by Goff.[47]

In announcing the beginning of the printed-card program

the previous year, Mr. Putnam had mentioned that the principal body of cards available was those for copyright books issued since 1897, and had suggested that copies of the *Catalog of Copyright Entries* might be used for ordering cards. The suggestion was not fruitful; after two years the Librarian reported: "The Catalogue of Copyright Entries seems to have proved to be an unsatisfactory means of ordering by serial numbers; apparently nothing short of a cumulative index would make it satisfactory for this purpose." [48] This could hardly have been surprising. It was taking librarians time to get used to the idea of ordering cards by card number when they habitually ordered books by author and title; the habit persisted for some time.

They were being aided by the card program—and by the copyright deposit system—in another way; it is doubtful if many librarians were ever really aware of this, or that they are now. The usefulness of the weekly copyright catalog in extending the coverage of the *American Catalogue* has been mentioned. After the inauguration of the card program Mr. Bowker also had the benefit of the cataloging work of the Library, for a free copy of each card for a copyright title was sent "in exchange" to *Publishers' Weekly*. Beginning June 1, 1902, the Library supplied a second set of cards on the same basis to the H. W. Wilson Company of Minneapolis.[49] Thus at this time one cataloging operation by the Library, in preparing the catalog entry for a copyright deposit, produced an entry used in both the Library's card catalogs and those of the Copyright Office, in the *Catalog of Copyright Entries,* and supplemented or supplied information to Bowker's *American Catalogue* and Wilson's *Cumulative Book Index.*

The picture of American bibliographical activity during this period would not be complete without further mention of the work of Halsey W. Wilson. From his experience as a small Minneapolis bookseller since 1889, he was encouraged to begin publishing a current book-trade bibliography by the discontinuance in 1895 of Leypoldt's experiment with semiannual numbers of the *American Catalogue,* which left only a weekly and an annual service (*Publishers' Weekly* and *American Catalogue*) available to booksellers and libraries.[50] The first issue of the monthly *Cumulative Book Index* appeared in February 1898.[51] By the middle of the year entries for new books were arranged in one alphabetical list under author, title, and subject. At first Wilson simply reprinted data taken from the current issues of *Publishers' Weekly*. Using entries in individual publishers' catalogs, he compiled a list of books in print,[52] including, of course, most of the entries which had appeared in his monthly catalogs, and published the first issue of the *United States Catalog* in the fall of 1899.[53] The first years were years of experiment and struggle, but the publication pattern that emerged—monthly issues, cumulating at intervals during the year, then into annual, biennial, and quadrennial or quinquennial cumulations, and ultimately into the *United States Catalog*, for those remaining in print—provided the American book trade and library profession with an indispensable resource. In 1903 the H. W. Wilson Company was incorporated and "claimed the distinction at this time of entering upon really serious bibliographical work." [54] The fact that free copies of Library of Congress printed cards were regularly sent to the company may account in part for the unequivocal nature of this claim.

Friends in Minneapolis were helpful to Wilson in the early days, particularly faculty members of the university and the then librarian of the Minneapolis Athenaeum, Herbert Putnam.[55] Wilson's position became substantially more secure in 1911. "He and R. R. Bowker," writes J. L. Lawlor, ". . . had been engaged in a polite form of warfare for more than a decade. . . . Necessity compelled a truce. . . . They agreed, therefore, to coordinate their activities," [56] Bowker continuing to be the book industry's principal source of information about new books at the time of publication and before, and Wilson providing coverage of United States book production through monthly catalogs plus cumulations. The building of the Wilson bibliographic empire was a remarkable achievement; the deposit and cataloging provisions of the copyright law indirectly contributed to the firm's success through the medium of the printed cards supplied by the Library.

Following the use of the copyright catalog in getting the printed-card program started, library officers other than those in the Copyright Office appear to have had little further relation to it. Mr. Putnam, reporting to the American Library Association in 1905 on the status of the Library as the national library, did not mention the *Catalog* at all, although he acknowledged the value of copyright deposits as one of the library's unique sources of acquisition, and as permitting appropriated funds to be expended for works not received by copyright or exchange.[57] He recognized that the cards distributed in the largest quantities through the card service were those for the "usual book," the book acquired by many libraries. Nevertheless, the principle that the cards were produced primarily for the Library itself, and that those supplied to other libraries were a "mere by-product," was now well established. While one of the functions of the Library, to supplement other collections "for research," required it to have the "unusual book," it must also have the "usual book" to make its card service useful to other libraries. "The distribution of its catalog cards, therefore, will tend to round out its collections in directions which mere research would not require or justify." [58] If the word "usual" was meant to be read to mean regular American trade books, most of which were received by copyright, he may have been suggesting that the copyright deposits were of more significance as the basis for the card distribution program than they were as additions to the Library collections. It perhaps is not to be wondered that he did not appear to join Bowker in proposing the further development of the bibliographic potential of the copyright catalog.

It is clear that Thorvald Solberg, however, not only continued to be responsive to proposals for increased bibliographic use, within limits, but also held firmly to the validity of issuing the *Catalog* to assist customs officers. Investigations within the Treasury Department had convinced the department that the

Catalog was not of sufficient help to customs officers in preventing the importation of foreign editions infringing works of American manufacture to warrant its continued publication by the Treasury. The Secretary of the Treasury, on January 16, 1904, recommended to Congress that responsibility for publication, as well as compilation, of the *Catalog* be centralized under the Librarian of Congress, maintaining, in justification, that the *Catalog* was not "at all helpful to the officers of the customs and postal services." [59] The Register of Copyrights was in agreement with the proposal to transfer publication of the *Catalog* to the Library, but was at a loss to understand how information could be supplied in more usable form.[60] In answer to the Treasury Department's criticism that the *Catalog* cost far more to publish than the small number of subscribers justified, the Register pointed out that the copyright fees might properly be considered an offset to its cost.

Mr. Solberg also took opportunity to describe some of the other uses of the *Catalog*. It was "the most available index to the copyright business" both in and out of the Copyright Office. It was employed both for administrative purposes and for answering the "thousands" of inquiries which came to the Office each year; for the latter purpose distribution as a public document would make the *Catalog* more useful. In the second place, it provided security against loss or destruction, "as the printed catalogue is virtually a transcript of the copyright record books, so far as all essential facts regarding any registration are concerned." And finally, the *Catalog* "is the official contemporaneous record of the literary, artistic, dramatic, and musical production of our country, and there seem many good reasons why such a record should be maintained." [61]

Responsibility for publication of the *Catalog* was transferred to the Library by the Sundry Civil Appropriation Act of June 30, 1906.[62] Solberg signaled the change in responsibility by changing the title to *Catalogue of Copyright Entries* (the "ue" was dropped in 1934), *New Series*, and by instituting other organizational changes which he hoped would make it more useful. The Library's annual report for 1907 describes them:

"Beginning with July 1, 1906 the Catalogue was divided in accordance with the subject matter of the articles registered. Thus, Part 1 now contains the titles of all copyright books, dramatic compositions, and maps and charts; Part 2 the titles of all periodicals registered for copyright protection; Part 3 the titles of all musical compositions so registered, and Part 4 all registrations under other designations provided by the copyright law, including works of the fine arts, engravings, chromos and lithographs, and photographs.

"In Part 1 of the Catalogue two groups are made of the book titles, one containing the titles of all books for which the Library of Congress supplies printed cards and the second containing titles of pamphlets, leaflets, and all other publications registered under the legal designation 'book.' The titles included in the first group are printed to correspond with the titles as printed on the Library of Congress cards, and for that purpose the linotype slugs now used in printing such cards are again used for the Catalogue, and the resetting of the titles is thus saved. The titles for pamphlets, leaflets, and other smaller publications registered under the legal designation 'book' are arranged in a monthly alphabet to save the necessity for searching fifty-two weekly alphabets for such titles. In the same way the titles for periodicals, engravings, cuts, prints, chromos, lithographs, etc., are cumulated for a monthly alphabet, so as to reduce the number of alphabets required to be searched to twelve each year for each class.

"The numbers printed for each of the four parts of the Catalogue are prepared for binding up at the end of the year into separate volumes, separately indexed, according to subject-matter, and separate subscriptions are taken for each of the four parts." [63]

At the outset the Copyright Office issued weekly catalogs in the case of each of the four parts. During the ensuing six months, however, this plan was abandoned in favor of monthly catalogs except for Part 1, the part devoted to books and pamphlets, dramas, and maps.

On July 2, 1906, exhibits of the new form of the *Catalog* were shown to the members of the Bibliographical Society of America, who pronounced it "a valuable piece of systematic bibliography." [64] Five days later Solberg stated, in a letter to James Bain, librarian of the Toronto Public Library, "I want to make it so complete a bibliographical record of copyright registrations that it will be indispensable to most libraries, and any suggestions from you in line with this end will be given careful consideration." [65] R. R. Bowker added his word: "Recognition should again be made of the remarkable work in bibliography now carried on by the Library of Congress, particularly through the printed records of the Copyright Office. As has already been suggested, it is not improbable that in view of the increasing product of the American press and the consequent strain upon the resources of private publication, private enterprises may ultimately be superseded by an official bibliography published by the national library, in which case the present volumes would be, in a sense, the initial portion of the continuous record of American bibliography." [66] Solberg and Bowker were apparently looking forward to the continued bibliographic development of the *Catalog of Copyright Entries.*

5 The Act of March 4, 1909

THE CATALOGING PROVISIONS OF THE MEMORANDUM DRAFT BILL OF OCTOBER 23, 1905

1. Development of the Draft Bill

The Act of March 4, 1909, was very largely the work of Thorvald Solberg. To refine it by exposure to the criticisms of representatives of the principal copyright industries and other persons concerned with copyright, Herbert Putnam with Solberg's assistance conducted three extended meetings in 1905 and 1906. Fortunately the sessions were recorded stenographically in full. The first one, held Wednesday through Friday, May 31-June 2, 1905, did not consider the cataloging provisions.

The following Monday Solberg formally requested leave of absence with pay for the period June 24-August 31 (which was to include his vacation) for "the framing of the proposed draft of a general copyright law." [1] The full, detailed draft bill which he produced was issued under date of October 23, 1905, and was sent the following day to those who were expected to attend the second conference. It was at this meeting, held November 1-4, 1905, that the principal comments on Solberg's cataloging provisions were heard. The third and final conference was March 13-16, 1906.

The persons attending and participating in these conferences included, in addition to Herbert Putnam and Thorvald Solberg and other government officers, representatives and legal counsel of authors' societies and copyright industries. In addition, representatives of the American Library Association and the National Education Association attended most of the sessions. Frank P. Hill, librarian of the Brooklyn Public Library and president of the American Library Association beginning in July 1905, and Arthur E. Bostwick, chief of the Circulation Department of the New York Public Library, represented the library group. Educational interests were represented by George S. Davis, associate city superintendent of schools of the District of Columbia, and Claude G. Leland, librarian of the Board of Education, City of New York.

2. *The Provisions in Detail*

In his opening remarks at the second conference Herbert Putnam stated that the draft reflected suggestions made during the first conference held in June, some specific suggestions which had been received by mail, and, for the rest, suggestions emanating from the Copyright Office as the result of its experience and studies.[2] Solberg had prepared a full draft, containing quite detailed statements of each provision, so that the conferees might have the fullest and clearest picture possible of all proposals. The cataloging provisions were embodied in sections 13 and 14 of the draft. Section 13 provided for:

1. The maintenance of a manuscript card catalog and index of all coypright registrations.
2. The production of a printed catalog, monthly or more frequently, containing the titles and descriptions of articles deposited and registered, so arranged as to conform best to the classes of the works deposited and to the uses of the catalog.
3. The production of complete and thorough printed quarterly indexes to the catalog.
4. The production of a printed annual index to the catalog.
5. The production of printed five-year complete catalogs, containing all entries for the period rearranged and indexed, in the case of books, dramas, and music.

6. The production of printed ten-year complete catalogs, containing all entries for the period rearranged and indexed, in the case of each of the other classes.
7. Upon publication of such cumulations, the destruction of the original manuscript cards represented in them.

Section 14 provided for:

1. The prompt distribution of the current catalogs to collectors of customs and postmasters of postoffices receiving foreign mails.
2. The furnishing to the Register of Copyrights by the Secretary of the Treasury and the Postmaster General of lists of such officers, revised quarterly.
3. The furnishing of the catalogs to all parties desiring them, at a price to be determined by the Register not exceeding five dollars a year for the complete catalog or one dollar a year for any one class.
4. The furnishing of the five- and ten-year catalogs to all persons ordering them at a price based on the regulations governing the price of public documents as of the date of issue.
5. The handling of the subscriptions for and the mailing of the current, five-year, and ten-year catalogs by the Superintendent of Documents.
6. The payment of moneys received from such subscriptions into the Treasury of the United States in accordance with regulations in force at any time.

It should be noted that Solberg visualized the continuance of a manuscript card catalog; a current printed catalog of works deposited and registered, issued at least monthly with complete quarterly and annual indexes; cumulated catalogs, rearranged and indexed, covering works deposited and registered during five- or ten-year periods, depending upon the class. His choosing of books, dramas, and music for the five-year cumulations suggest that he was taking into account both the size of the classes and the relative amount of public interest in them. He provided for inclusion in the catalogs of works "deposited and registered." He recognized the problem of searching through many issues of frequently published lists by providing for quarterly and annual indexes. Thus the "current" catalogs, while basically monthly in concept, were planned for effective use in searches covering three-, six-, nine-, and twelve-month periods. The five- and ten-year catalogs were clearly designed to replace not only the manuscript cards but also the "current" catalogs; they were to be "complete, rearranged, and indexed."

It is of some significance to note, also, that while provision was made for the distribution of the current as well as of the five- and ten-year catalogs "to all parties desiring them" and "to all persons ordering them," only the current catalogs were to be supplied to the collectors of customs and postmasters. It is not clear whether the quarterly and annual indexes were meant to be included in this distribution, although they would surely have been as useful to the collectors of customs and postmasters as to any other searcher. It would seem to be clear, however, that the cumulative catalogs were intended for general public use rather than for the specialized use of the customs officers and postmasters.

3. *Relevance of the Provisions to Anticipated Uses of the* Catalog

Solberg's draft bill does not clearly and specifically provide a rationale for the particulars contained in these provisions. His most revealing contemporary statement explaining the purposes of the *Catalog* as he conceived them was contained in his reply, early in 1904, to the Secretary of the Treasury's criticism of its usefulness as a means of preventing importation of piratical works.[3] As has been indicated, he felt the criticism was unwarranted, and gave the following as the *Catalog*'s basic functions:

1. A copyright search tool for customs officers and postmasters.
2. A convenient copyright search tool for the public and the Copyright Office staff.
3. A means of making the copyright record secure.
4. The official national bibliographic record.

The first two of these functions are clearly accounted for in the draft bill, the third by the provisions for printing and distribution, the fourth principally by the provision for quarterly and annual indexes and the cumulations, and also by the fact that, as had been the case since 1891, the entries were to be of works deposited as well as registered, and thus a catalog of works physically existing.

DISCUSSION OF THE CATALOGING PROVISIONS

Some further light on Solberg's concept of the *Catalog of Copyright Entries* is discernible in his presentation of sections 13 and 14 of the draft bill to the second copyright conference in November 1905, and in the discussion which followed. This took place on Thursday afternoon, November 2, with the representatives of the American Library Association, Frank P. Hill and Arthur E. Bostwick, present but silent.[1] Hill and Bostwick had been far from silent in the morning session, however, having argued at length, with George Haven Putnam the principal adversary, for retention in the law of the exception to the non-importation provision permitting libraries to have a limited but free access to British editions of works copyrighted in the United States, without the necessity of first securing permission from the licensee of United States book rights.[2] The American Library Association representatives, in reporting back to the association's executive board, suggested possible compromises; when these were aired, strong opposition to compromise of any sort developed among many librarians. Led by Bernard C. Steiner of Baltimore and W. P. Cutter of Northampton, Massachusetts, the Library Copyright League was formed to fight for a more unequivocal provision,[3] rather than for one of the several compromise positions which the association advanced at various times. The strength of feeling on this point, both within the library profession and between librarians and publishers, kept the attention of the profession focused upon importation as virtually the sole copyright problem of interest to librarians, both prior to 1909 and for many years to come.

In the afternoon session Solberg expressed his hope that there would be full discussion of the various administrative provisions since most of them were new to the statute. "To some of these we attach considerable importance . . ."; one of these, for example, was the provision "that there shall be maintained the publication of the *Catalogue of Copyright Entries.* Now it is no secret that in the commendable attempt at economy in public administration, that document will be scrutinized with other current governmental publications, and the question raised whether it is serving a sufficiently useful purpose to justify its continuation at the expense [sic]. It would, therefore, make a difference whether the people who are interested in copyright property would be on record as expressing their desire that this should continue for a good purpose." [4] This statement can only mean that Solberg wished the publication to continue, but that it might not unless it was supported by the copyright industries.

He reviewed other administrative provisions on which he wished discussion, including that relating to the record books. He called attention to the fact that his draft provision deviated from the specificity of the existing law and left "it open to the Register to devise such form as he can most economicaly [sic] and rationally provide." [5] At this point Bowker interposed a question which placed the discussion on a desirably broad basis since it was directed not simply to the printed *Catalog* but to the whole question of the extent to which the Copyright Office should provide indexes to the record. Should it go so far, for example, as to reveal the relationships of subsidiary copyrights to original works, specifying all the transfers of rights which had been granted? Charles W. Ames, representing United Typothetae of America, also expressed interest in this question.[6]

Solberg's response revealed his belief that a service of this magnitude was not to be contemplated: "I think you have raised a very broad question, and the Office has been obliged to say that certain registrations and certain clues to registrations are not required by the present law, and there is no provision to meet them. Now it is a question whether it ought to be a burden upon the Copyright Office; for example, until there is a law to give a monopoly in the use of a title, it does not seem to be a proper burden upon the Copyright Office to be able to answer as to whether a certain title has been used or not; that is a constant inquiry and a constant source of criticism, if not complaint, that it cannot be done. The question at once arises should the Copyright Office be burdened with the preparation and the carrying on of an index which would answer such questions? Now, possibly in line with Mr. Bowker's suggestion, if there are registrations made with a view to keeping the subsidiary rights with the elemental or fundamental rights, it would certainly involve a considerable additional burden on the Office. It would always be incomplete, and it would be of qualified value, because it is incomplete, in that it does not go back. Then, is the Copyright Office to be charged with going back and completing the indexes? Where the registrations run as high as 100,000 and more per year—and they will soon be 150,000—the index question is really a serious one, and it ought to be kept in one's mind in relation to the fee." [7]

The representative of the International Typographical Union, J. J. Sullivan, suggested the Register should have authority "to make such rules as are necessary"; and Karl Bitter of the National Sculpture Society expressed the view that "the Copyright Office should be obliged to give any reasonable information that it is asked to give." Mr. Solberg made it clear that he believed the law should contain something that would give the Register authority to publish a catalog but that would also impel Congress "to provide means." He accepted as a "well-established practice that in any office of record any question as to the facts recorded in the office are [sic] at the disposal of the public." [8]

However, there were limits to what the Office should be expected to do: "if a person for his private reasons wants a long investigation on a general subject, and not on a specific registration, he is either to be charged a fee for the service, or he is to be permitted to do it himself." And, of course, the Office could not give legal advice or attempt to interpret the statute.[9]

W. A. Livingstone, representing the Print Publishers' Association of America, raised a specific question as to whether the Office should undertake to determine for a client whether or not a specific title had previously been used. Solberg's reply revealed how the Office had so far interpreted its responsibilities:

"Would the office be properly charged to ascertain whether any title had been recorded, or what descriptions had been recorded under a given form of title? It is clearly a pertinent question to have an expression of opinion upon, and I would like to say right here, without taking too much time, that in line with that, the question may be asked what should be the final point of indexing. Now the practice of the office from the beginning has been that, first, there should be a clue from every claimant of copyright, original claimant of copyright. This bill goes a little farther and provides for an index from the claimant under a transference of copyright. Then the office, trying in the later years to act upon practical hard sense, asks itself from what other initial point do the most inquiries come. We find that in the case of dramas the constant inquiry is regarding the title. While the office has taken the position that it is not legally required to index titles as such, as a convenience to the office in answering inquiries to a reasonable extent, the dramatic compositions are indexed under the titles, in addition to the proprietors. That has also been extended to the indexing of the titles of musical compositions, because there again the constant inquiry is for the title; and to economize on the other side we have made a primary registration under the title in the case of the periodical, because it is hardly ever the question of the proprietor of a periodical. . . ." [10]

At this point the representative of the Reproductive Arts Copyright League, Edmund B. Osborne, presented a rationale of the problem that appears to have escaped Mr. Solberg. Osborne pointed out that the purpose of the indexing function was "to protect two classes of people; first, to protect those who make original works, and secondly to protect any one, the public, . . . publishers, or others who do not want to be pirates." Careless as to metaphor but clear as to meaning, he went on: "To keep them from doing a thing which they do not intend to do and to enable them to steer clear of the rocks, the one thing necessary is that you get a hook in somewhere to get identification. If I have got the author's name, or the publisher's name, I should be able to get in there and get final information." [11] It should be noted that Osborne stressed the need for access to the record through the names of authors and publishers, whereas Solberg had clearly indicated he had been pushed into providing title access, in addition to proprietor, only as the result of experience in handling the inquiries that came to the Office.

Despite his acceptance of the principle that the facts of record were at the disposal of the public, Solberg was dubious as to the degree to which they should be available and as to the extent to which the Office should be prepared to assist searchers for these facts, or to perform searches on behalf of others. Although it was anticipated that many copyright deposit copies would be retained by the Copyright Office when they had not been selected for the collections of the Library of Congress, a patron's request to examine one of these copies would be "an encroachment upon the office service," and, in such cases, "it would be well . . . to make sure there should be an adequate reason for the search"; ordinarily, the patron would be expected to consult the work in the Reading Room of the Library.[12]

One comes inescapably to the conclusion that Solberg wished to avoid making a public copyright reference center of the Copyright Office. While he subscribed to the theory of public access to the record, he wished to provide it through the printed, disseminated catalog, rather than through the "manuscript card files," record books, and deposits retained in the Office. He seems to have had little faith in the continued efficiency of the card files, and proposed the printing of five- and ten-year catalogs "to relieve the great accumulation of cards which would be unmanageable, so that those cards could be destroyed." [13] The fact that he had instituted title entry for certain classes of material indicated that he was responsive to the ways in which information was looked for, but nevertheless was constrained always to provide an approach by copyright proprietor (except for books and periodicals); Osborne's plea for additional entries under author and publisher as a regular practice appears to have been a new idea altogether.

Charles W. Ames proposed that the sense of the discussion be recorded as "that the records . . . should be so indexed as to give access to all the facts, [including renewals and transfers and the like,] recorded in connection with each particular article deposited." Both Ames and Bowker had made this proposition before. Solberg dismissed it now as "not something to be accomplished. . . . In dealing with such large masses some common sense has to be used. We can give the reasonable points of inquiry, such as the proprietor's name, the author of the book, the title of the drama, the title of the music, and the artist's name in relation to works of art, and possibly some other data." [14]

Solberg did not commit himself clearly on the question of fullness of indexing, although he did as to exactness: "If the office is to become what the bill really leans to, a final office of record for titles to literary and artistic property, the more exact the registration and indexing can be made the better." [15]

When the discussion turned to making the *Catalog of Copyright Entries* prima facie evidence of the facts stated therein, Solberg pointed out that under the new law there would be no essential change in the content of the catalogs. "The only change would be made from the record form to the bibliographical form, but the same facts would appear in the case of each entry." He also reminded the group of the value of the printed catalogs as insurance against loss or destruction of the record, and as a convenience in conducting searches involving a great many entries.[16]

The sections of Solberg's draft bill relating to importation of unauthorized copies were considered on Saturday morning, November 4. The representative of the Treasury Department,

Charles P. Montgomery, in reviewing existing procedures of customs officers, stated they could know that an article was prohibited from entry under the copyright law only when it bore a notice of copyright or when the officer could locate the work in the *Catalog of Copyright Entries*. "This latter is a physical impossibility . . ." [17]

"When an importation arrives marked with the United States notice of copyright, the customs officers readily detect the irregularity, but when an importation comes in bearing no notice of copyright, the customs officers cannot hold up such importation long enough to go through the million and a half title entries in order to determine whether the article is prohibited.

"An effort has been made to devise some scheme which may give you the protection the law wants, and as a substitute for the catalogue of title entries, but none has been found . . ." [18]

In the brief discussion which followed Mr. Montgomery's statement interest was expressed in the desirability of the objective, but no suggestions for improving the customs procedures were forthcoming. Solberg requested that suggestions be sent him for making the Catalog more useful.[19]

Solberg's draft bill had intentionally been prepared in very great detail in order to present all the issues clearly. Richard Rogers Bowker had argued strongly at the beginning of this series of meetings against retaining such particularized language, as providing too much opportunity for loopholes to appear in time where none were intended.[20]

Upon the basis of the suggestions made in these conferences new bills were prepared in briefer form and introduced into Congress. Hearings were held on S. 6330 and H.R. 19853 by the Joint Committee on Patents in June and December 1906 and in March 1908. In these hearings the *Catalog of Copyright Entries* elicited very little comment. The Treasury Department stated again its view that the *Catalog* was an impractical tool for the customs officers and postmasters to use.[24] H. N. Low of Washington, D.C., worried about the provision permitting the Register to destroy cards upon the issuance of "complete and indexed" catalogs:

Mr. Low. It appears to me that card indexes are very valuable, and much easier to consult than the printed volumes successively printed, and that they should be preserved in any way possible.

The Librarian. This is the opinion of the copyright office; that so long as the card indexes did not become unwieldy they should be preserved. We recognize that in the library proper, where we maintain our catalogue in the card form and extend it indefinitely. On the other hand, the card indexes of the copyright may become so distended that it will not be practicable there, in connection with other administrative work, to justify the retention of them when the matter of them has appeared in available printed form. The provision, however, only authorizes destruction. It does not require it.[22]

Other than this there was no discussion of the *Catalog* provision. Solberg's new draft had effectively reduced argument. There is no reason to believe the textual changes materially altered his concept of the kind of catalog that should be published. To suggest, however, that this new condensed draft retained the clarity of the original draft would be quite incorrect. Since the further changes effected in the final stages of enactment of the Act of March 4, 1909, were of a minor character, it will suffice here to compare briefly the wording of the cataloging provisions in the act as passed with that distributed by Solberg on October 23, 1905.

THE CATALOGING PROVISIONS AS ADOPTED

Sections 13 and 14 of the draft bill became sections 56 and 57 in the Act of March 4, 1909. The principal differences between them are the following:

1. Section 56 of the act dropped the specific provision that a manuscript card catalog be maintained, but mentioned it in the provision authorizing the Register to "destroy the original manuscript catalogue cards," if expedient, upon the issuance of printed cumulative catalogs.

2. It introduced the words "shall fully index" as a general provision and added assignments to "all copyright registrations" as records to be indexed.
3. Instead of specifying the intervals of publication and the kind of publication to be issued at each interval ("the titles and descriptions of articles deposited and registered" at least monthly, "complete and thorough indexes" each quarter and annually, and "rearranged and indexed catalogues" at intervals of five or ten years, depending upon the class), the section condensed these specifications into "shall print at periodic intervals a catalogue of the titles of articles deposited and registered for copyright, together with suitable indexes," to govern the current catalogs, and "at stated intervals shall print complete and indexed catalogues for each class," to govern the cumulative catalogs.
4. It added the provision that the catalogs "shall be admitted in any court as *prima facie* evidence of the facts stated therein."
5. Section 57 referred only to "the said printed current catalogues" and to "the consolidated catalogues and indexes." The latter phrase replaced the original wording: "The five-year and ten-year consolidated catalogues and indexes."

While section 57 was otherwise somewhat abbreviated over its original form, there was no change in its intent.

Fees for making searches of copyright records had been charged prior to 1909 but were provided for in the law for the first time in the Act of 1909. The act also for the first time "introduced the provision that copyright records shall be open for public inspection." [1]

It would be wrong to say that sections 56 and 57 were models of condensation from Solberg's original draft. It is true the abbreviated and more general language gave the Register his authority to publish catalogs and something to impel Congress to provide the means, and at the same time gave him greater latitude in developing cataloging operations. Unfortunately, it also beclouded the purposes for which the *Catalog* was intended. There is no question but that Solberg was personally interested in and proud of the *Catalog*, as much for the reason of its contribution to national bibliography as any other. He did not have a concept of the Copyright Office as being an agency to service the record; he made no effort to provide a reference staff to serve the public, he was adamantly against giving service to mere curiosity seekers, and even to those desiring title searches, and he clearly considered it beyond his obligation as Register (if not actually impossible) to provide the means for determining relationships between original registrations and subsequent transfers of derivative rights. He persisted (with the support of the publishers) in retaining the provision for distributing the current catalogs to customs officers, in spite of repeated private and public statements of representatives of the Secretary of the Treasury that they were useless for the purpose intended. The merely oblique mention of the manuscript card catalog as against the predominance of the printed catalog in these two sections suggests strongly his overriding interest in the *Catalog of Copyright Entries* as a bibliography and as a copyright reference tool rather than in the maintenance of a card catalog designed for public use.

It is clear from section 57 that both the current and the cumulative catalogs were intended for distribution to and use by the public. Only the current catalogs were, in addition, to be distributed automatically to the customs officers and postmasters.

6 Operations Under the Cataloging Provisions of the Act of 1909 Through World War II

The Act of March 4, 1909, enabled Solberg to continue issuing the *Catalog of Copyright Entries* in the improved form he had developed after responsibility for the printing had been transferred from the Treasury Department in 1906. Basically it was a monthly catalog (except for the part devoted to books), with annual indexes, of works registered and deposited, and of renewal registrations beginning in 1909. Notices of use were included in the music catalog until 1927 but not thereafter. Assignment records were not included.

Special attention continued to be given to the part of the *Catalog* devoted to "books proper." These were the books selected currently to receive printed-card cataloging and, by and large, were the books transferred immediately to the collections of the Library for its use. The catalog entries were prepared by the Library's Catalogue Division and were reproduced in their entirety, and with the addition of the copyright facts supplied by Copyright Office personnel, in the part of the copyright catalog devoted to them. Other book materials not selected for such full cataloging treatment (by modern standards very full indeed) and the materials registered in all other copyright classes were cataloged by the Copyright Office staff.

To meet demands for promptness of information the "books proper" part of the *Catalog* was issued weekly—at certain periods two and three times a week. To meet another need of users the retail price of copyrighted books was included in the catalog entry; the information was secured by a request incorporated in the copyright application form.[1]

In effect, Solberg was providing the nation with a current, comprehensive national bibliography of books on a weekly, monthly, and annual basis, a bibliography that was also the copyright record of "books proper" in published form. In the other parts of the *Catalog* he was issuing a current complete record of works registered and deposited for copyright and renewed, on a monthly and annual basis. It is evident that neither bibliographers nor librarians, nor the officers of the Library of Congress itself, attached very much significance to the records of anything other than books.

The Library's card distribution activities were achieving success and recognition. The card catalog was, in the minds of librarians, the ultimate library tool and the catalog in book form a relic of the past. The copyright law required the Copyright Office to publish a catalog; close collaboration made it possible for the Library to contribute to this catalog the careful and skilled attention of its cataloging staff and to secure comprehensive coverage of American book production through both the printed card and the printed catalog. In both forms the Library was making a valuable contribution to American national bibliography on a level comparable to that then being achieved in England, France, and Germany.[2]

The effort required to make this arrangement work was prodigious, and the Copyright Office was under heavy pressure, exerted principally by C. H. Hastings of the Card Section,[3] to expedite the delivery of copyrighted books to the Library as soon as possible after receipt. Solberg was moved to describe publicly the efforts of the Copyright Office to accomplish the desired objective: "With a view to supply librarians and other users of the Catalogue with early information of all copyrighted books, special efforts have been made to forward promptly to the Catalogue Division for printed titles such books as have been deposited in the Copyright Office. In the case of a certain number of these, it has been found necessary to hold the copies pending correspondence with the depositors. From November 8, 1909 to June 30, 1910, inclusive, these delayed books numbered 1,338; but the remaining 6,916 books received were forwarded to the Library on the day of their receipt in the Copyright Office." [4]

The following year he felt constrained to describe the process in detail: "All books included in the Catalogue of Copyright Entries for which printed cards are made are catalogued by the Catalogue Division of the Library of Congress. The cards are printed first and the linotype slugs are at once used for the Catalogue of Copyright Entries, thus saving the cost of resetting. To avoid delay special effort is made to forward promptly the books deposited, and 11,400 books and pamphlets were delivered to the Catalogue Division during the fiscal year on the actual day of their receipt in the Copyright Office. The Catalogue Division titles are returned to the Copyright Office in 18 days, on an average, and as soon as enough titles are received to make up not less than 4 full pages of the catalogue, they are sent to the printer. By this method two or three numbers of the catalogue of books are printed and distributed each week instead of one weekly number as heretofore, and not only is a much more prompt distribution of the catalogue thus secured, but a considerable economy in printing as well. All blank or partly blank pages are eliminated and the printing of the 52 weekly title covers is saved. The monthly indexes are printed in separate numbers which contain also the lists of copyright renewals and any miscellaneous text matter, such as copyright proclamations, notices, etc. Each printed signature contains the actual date of printing and is given a consecutive number. The pages are numbered consecutively, as well as the titles, to make one yearly volume of solid bibliographical text. A complete yearly index of authors and proprietors is supplied for each volume to take the place of the monthly indexes when the catalogue is bound.

"The considerable deposit of foreign books made under the operation of the present copyright law adds a new element of value to the Catalogue of Copyright Books. A number of the current books and dramas printed and published in the leading countries of Europe are included, and it is believed librarians and others will appreciate the opportunity offered for receiving prompt bibliographical information concerning these works." [5]

The focus of these efforts was clearly on the American librarian, clearly not on the owners of copyright properties.

Authority to produce "complete and indexed" catalogs at "stated intervals" had been given to the Register in the Act of 1909. The first fruit of this provision was the publication, in 1916 and 1918, of *Dramatic Compositions Copyrighted in the United States, 1870 to 1916* in two fat volumes containing 3,547 pages and listing 56,066 works. In the preface to this cumulative catalog, Solberg stated that it had been planned many years earlier, and that one thousand copies had been printed and priced in accordance with the provisions relating to the "consolidated" catalogs. The price of the catalog was, and still is, $4.00 for the set. The final work of compilation and editing was done under the direction of Henry S. Parsons, who became chief of the Catalogue and Index Division of the Copyright Office on July 1, 1913. The division at this time had a staff of twenty-five.[6]

Production of the cumulative drama catalog had been a long chore and the publication was not conspicuously successful. Thirty years elapsed before another cumulation was attempted.

Appropriations for printing the *Catalog of Copyright Entries* at this time were included in a blanket appropriation covering all of the Library's printing. From the Register's point of view this presented some problems, especially when he did not receive from the Library what he considered was necessary to ensure prompt publication of the *Catalog*. Ligon Johnson of New York, who had developed a specialized reference service reporting on copyright claims, was a frequent complainant about the delays in publication. In 1923, four days after attempting to mollify Mr. Johnson,[7] Solberg wrote Bowker:

"Our Copyright Catalogue is nearly a half year in arrears, and while I was away the printing was stopped practically entirely, only the printing of the leaflets for books proper being allowed to proceed. We have been the recipients of very severe criticism for this delay in supplying the Catalogue. The printing appropriation is made in a lump sum, but it states specifically that it is to cover the printing for the Copyright Office, including the Catalogue of Copyright Entries. Now, however, Mr. Boyd [chief clerk of the Library of Congress] has sent me notice that of the total appropriation of $213,000 for printing for this fiscal year, only $25,000 will be allotted for the printing of the Catalogue of Copyright Entries. As the cost of printing the Catalogue last year amounted to nearly $30,000, that is tantamount to saying that the Catalogue can be printed for ten months only instead of twelve months. My contention is that the law is mandatory . . ." [8]

Feeling that the *Catalog* was in danger, Solberg rose to its defense publicly, restating its purposes in clear terms:

"The copyright act of March 4, 1909, provides 'that the register of copyrights shall fully index all copyright registrations and assignments,' and it further provides that the register of copyrights 'shall print at periodic intervals a catalogue of the titles of articles deposited and registered for copyright, together with suitable indexes . . .'

"Strenuous efforts are made in the copyright office to carry out these provisions of law and to keep the index of copyright entries sharply up to date, in order to be able to promptly and accurately answer the daily inquiries in relation to any copyright entry actually made, received by mail or telegraph, or on personal application. Moreover, this catalogue constitutes the only complete and adequate current record published of the literary, musical, dramatic, and artistic productions of the United States, including also a record of similar foreign productions, to the extent to which foreign books, music, dramas, and works of art are deposited and registered in the copyright office.

"The preparation and publication of the catalogue has been planned with great care and with a desire to make it, what the law clearly contemplates, a complete record, and to make sure that the printed parts of the catalogue are so regularly and promptly distributed as to satisfactorily serve the needs, not only of the Government officials in whose behalf it is primarily provided to enable them to protect the interests of copyright claimants against importation of pirated copies, but to serve the needs of all libraries, and of the larger publishers of American copyright material, and of paid subscribers to the catalogue.

"From year to year the catalogue has been prepared and has been printed with commendable promptness and regularity, and this has been greatly appreciated. The value of the catalogue to regular users is directly proportionate to the promptness and regularity with which it is available for use. The discussions on the copyright bill brought out clearly the importance attached to the immediate availability of knowledge of copyright registrations, especially by motion-picture producers, phonograph-record makers, and broadcasters.

"The lack of sufficient printing funds occasions, at times, a delay in the publication of certain of the numbers of the catalogue. This is apt to occur, especially at the end of the fiscal year. However, it is hoped that as a result of representations the necessary appropriation may be made to provide for the prompt issuance of the numbers." [9]

Solberg, while now past seventy, was immersed in a drive to secure legislation which would permit the United States to join the Berne Union. In this effort he was working closely with George Haven Putnam (now eighty-one) and R. R. Bowker (now seventy-seven). The old battle between the librarians (represented now by M. Llewellyn Raney of the University of Chicago Library) and the publishers (represented by G. H. Putnam) still raged fiercely. Referring to a draft bill prepared to permit United States adherence to the International Copyright Union and ready for introduction, Solberg wrote to an old friend: "The publishers want to use the opportunity to add a privilege for their special benefit, namely, the absolute control of importation, practically the prohibition of importation of competing copies. The librarians, of course, have been up in arms against this for some time, and it is not very clear how they could be expected to waive their objection. They carry with them, no doubt, the educational institutions and I suppose the public, so far as it has in any way caught on to the proposal. . . ." [10]

Solberg's efforts to reconcile opposing views so that the United States could join the Berne Union were generally fruitless and led him to the point of wondering whether the solution might not be in proposing a bill "*simply* to enable the United States to enter the Copyright Union, leaving out of it all details." He brought the idea to the attention of Herbert Putnam: "He made neither reply nor comment—other than what might be implied in his startled look. I think he might be induced to agree. I really doubt our 'arriving' otherwise." [11]

It is also evident that Solberg was ready to give up all the formalities that had been characteristic of the United States system for so long. He asked Bowker about George Haven Putnam's desire to retain deposit and registration in the United States law; he knew Mr. Putnam "was at one time very much in earnest about the necessity but it seems as if that is one of the requirements that the United States will be obliged to abandon, as practically all other nations have." [12] Abandonment of the system of deposit and registration would also have meant automatic discontinuance of the *Catalog of Copyright Entries.* Solberg was thus prepared to see the elimination of the official copyright record and of a deposit system dependent upon copyright, together with an inevitable dislocation (at the least) of the existing national bibliographical structure.

The widespread desire to secure legislation enabling the United States to join the Berne Union prompted the introduction into Congress, between 1924 and 1940, of several bills, each of which amounted to a general revision of the copyright law. All of these bills attempted to compromise the problem of formalities yet continue to make provision for registration, deposit, and the publication of the copyright record. They differed from each other with respect to the cataloging provisions, principally in the extent to which they described the cataloging operation and in the way in which certain problems were to be resolved.

Of the six major bills, for example, four (Dallinger,[13] Sirovich,[14] Duffy,[15] Thomas[16]) provided for the continued distribution of the current catalogs to customs officers, two (Sirovich, Duffy) for the destruction of manuscript catalog cards on the completion of consolidated catalogs, four (Dallinger, Vestal,[17] Sirovich, Thomas) for indexing by author in addition to title, four (Dallinger, Perkins,[18] Sirovich, Duffy) for the admission of the catalogs as prima facie evidence of the facts stated therein, two (Dallinger, Thomas) for the inclusion of transfers and grants in the printed catalogs, five (Dallinger, Perkins, Vestal, Sirovich, Duffy) for the printing of "complete" cumulative catalogs, and one (Thomas) for the printing of monthly and annual catalogs only. All of the bills tended to assume that the purpose of a published catalog was to serve as the principal copyright reference tool. There does not appear to have been any real consideration of other possible uses. None of the bills was enacted into law.[19]

During the time these efforts were being made to revise the law, the regular work of the Copyright Office continued with relatively little change. Finally, after thirty-three years as Register, Mr. Solberg retired, choosing his seventy-eighth birthday, April 22, 1930, for the occasion. He was succeeded by William L. Brown, who served as Acting Register for four years, then as Register until July 31, 1936. Brown was followed by Col. Clement L. Bouvé for the period 1936-43. Both had not only to contend with general revision proposals but also to keep the Office operating effectively under the handicaps imposed by the depression. World War II heightened these problems, and the *Catalog of Copyright Entries* became a major casualty. Reductions in printing funds required taking drastic measures to reduce costs. While the complete *Catalog* continued to be issued, as the law required, the entries and indexes were reduced to bare essentials.

By the end of World War II the *Catalog of Copyright Entries* had largely lost its usefulness as a national bibliography and was the cause of much dissatisfaction on the part of its "hard core" users: a few publishers (principally of music), performing rights societies, authors' and composers' organizations, and the specialized copyright search firms. The library world and the book trade had effective services available to them in the weekly lists of new books in *Publishers' Weekly*, the monthly issues of Wilson's *Cumulative Book Index*, cumulating frequently up to quadrennial issues, and Bowker's annual lists of books in print. No services clearly comparable to these, however, were available for cultural materials other than books, except in the issues of the *Catalog of Copyright Entries.*

When Solberg had occasion, several years after his retirement, to review his contributions as Register, he placed the *Catalog* high among his accomplishments: "The extensive Catalogue of Copyright Entries from 1898 to date, now containing very many volumes, was my individual, personal creation. It is, I think, not matched as a National record of the literary, musical and dramatic output of any country. It has been issued in parts, usually weekly or monthly, but in the case of books, twice weekly. Another bibliographical work carried out under my planning and direction is a Catalogue of Copyrighted Dramas, from 1870 to 1916. It contains more than 56,000 titles of dramatic compositions with careful index, 3,500 pages in two quarto volumes." [20] In defending the *Catalog* against the criticisms of the Treasury Department in 1904 he had upheld its use, as we have seen, for preventing illegal importations from entering the country and had pointed to its value as a means of making the copyright record secure, as a tool facilitating searches for copyright information by the Copyright Office and the public, and as the national record of intellectual production. Whatever his personal convictions may have been during his years as Register of Copyrights, Thorvald Solberg in retirement thought of the *Catalog of Copyright Entries* as being, first of all, the official United States record of the intellectual works of the nation. In this view he was in the worthy company of William Elliot, Charles Coffin Jewett, Ainsworth Rand Spofford, and Richard Rogers Bowker.

Postscript

The end of World War II opened the way for the channeling of talent, money, and energy into new and expanded activities in all peacetime endeavors. Machines and techniques developed during the war were now applied to nonmilitary problems as well as military, and the urgencies typical of wartime carried over to problems of rebuilding and converting to more normal conditions. The industries supplying the materials of communication expanded or changed direction as new forms were invented and new interests developed. As the new forms of communication increased the rapidity with which the distance between sender and receiver could be covered, it became not only easier to communicate with other lands but compellingly necessary to do so. National movements became world movements, and national interest hardly distinguishable from international interest.

One of these movements was to culminate in the Universal Copyright Convention, which the United States ratified in 1955. Most of the major countries producing intellectual works in quantity are now members. Because the convention was built on the principle of national treatment—each nation offering to foreign authors the same protection given its own—the formalities of notice, deposit, and registration, which have been characteristic of the United States copyright system for so long, have not been the insurmountable obstacle to international copyright relations that they were when efforts were being made to join the Berne Union in the twenties and thirties.

The development of expanded markets for creative works, especially those required by the newer media of communication, brought fresh opportunities for creators and gave rise to new problems for the producers and distributors of works, who still had often to labor under antiquated national copyright laws.

In varying degrees this was true of all major countries. Aggressive action on a world basis to modernize these laws and establish new trade relationships was needed; such action has been, and is being, successfully undertaken. In the United States a program of research which looks toward the early accomplishment of a general revision of its more than fifty-year-old law has been in progress during the past few years.

A concomitant need to bring improvement to existing bibliographical devices used for the dissemination of information about intellectual works and for controlling these works when organized into collections has also become urgent. Notable responses to this need have been made in many parts of the world. In the United States these responses have come from diverse worlds: from librarians, scholars, electronics engineers, scientists and technicians, from government, and from the trades. Coordination of the activities of these groups has to a considerable extent been haphazard, it is true; it is probably correct to say, however, that the Library of Congress has been a major cohesive force in these efforts. Its unique capacity, by virtue of depository laws and world-wide governmental exchange arrangements, to secure reasonably comprehensive coverage of the intellectual materials of the world in all forms, and thus to be the nation's central agency for making the bibliographical record of them, underlies much of the bibliographical structure of the United States and influences, at the very least, the nature of comparable services in other parts of the world. The copyright law, through its provisions for deposit of copies and for making and preserving a record of the works deposited, forms an important segment of the structure.

Librarians of research libraries have been concerned that their collections not only have outgrown available accommodations but have become unwieldy to service simply because of their size. This problem of size has extended even to card catalogs, as Thorvald Solberg anticipated, and has prompted investigations into alternatives to their continued expansion. Catalogs in book form make dissemination possible, but they rarely constitute a substitute for the card catalog. Publication of catalogs in book form almost inevitably means a multiplication of alphabets, a loss of index approaches, or a very costly cumulative program, whereas the card catalog provides the convenience and the surety that only a tool in one alphabet can give. These problems and the related problem of bibliographical description are being widely studied in the United States and by cooperating groups in other parts of the world.

The relationships between these movements and developments in the recording operations of the Copyright Office in recent years cannot easily be reported as yet. The elements have been too much in flux and the perspective too restricted to make feasible a thorough historical analysis of the years that have elapsed since Thorvald Solberg's retirement. The events reviewed here, however, would seem to have some relevance to the resolution of problems now being given wide attention, problems which somehow appear to be much the same, in their essentials, as those of a half century ago.

Notes

CHAPTER 2 PREDECESSORS OF THE CATALOG OF COPYRIGHT ENTRIES

General Background

1. Hellmut Lehmann-Haupt, *The Book in America* (2d ed. New York, R. R. Bowker, 1951), pp. 123-24.

2. Ibid., pp. 119-263.

3. *A Catalogue of Books Published in America, and for Sale at the Bookstore of John West* was printed by Samuel Etheridge in 1797 (cited in Lehmann-Haupt, p. 133). The 1804 list, *Catalogue of All the Books, Printed in the United States, with the prices, and places where published, annexed,* is reproduced in Adolf Growoll, *Book-Trade Bibliography in the United States in the 19th Century* (Didbin Club, 1898).

4. Growoll, p. xviii.

5. Ibid., p. xx.

6. Constance M. Winchell, *Guide to Reference Books* (7th ed. Chicago, American Library Association, 1951), p. 20.

7. Growoll, p. xxi.

8. Henry Bartlett Van Hoesen, *Bibliography, Practical, Enumerative, Historical* (New York, Scribner, 1928), pp. 221-22.

9. Ibid., p. 222.

10. *Extracts from the Diaries and Accounts of Isaiah Thomas from the Year 1782 to 1804 and His Diary for 1808,* ed. Charles L. Nicholas. American Antiquarian Society *Proceedings, N.S. 26* (Worcester, American Antiquarian Society, 1916), 69.

11. Isaiah Thomas, *The History of Printing in America* (2d ed. 2 vols. Albany, Joel Munsell, 1874), *1,* x-xi.

12. Benjamin Franklin Thomas, "Memoir of Isaiah Thomas," in ibid., *1,* lxxxiii.

13. Isaiah Thomas, *1,* xii.

14. Winchell, p. 20.

15. See, for example, Evans 30122, 31193, 32460, 33855.

16. Library of Congress, Letter Book, 1843-1849.

17. Smithsonian Institution, *Annual Report . . . 1848,* pp. 17, 55-60.

18. Library of Congress, Letter Book.

19. Growoll, p. xxi.

20. Winchell, p. 20.

Elliot's List of Patents Granted by the United States

1. Martin A. Roberts, *Records in the Copyright Office Deposited by the United States District Courts Covering the Period 1790-1870* ([Washington], Government Printing Office, 1939), p. 12.

2. *A List of Patents Granted by the United States, for the Encouragement of Arts and Sciences, alphabetically arranged, from 1790 to 1820; containing the names of the patentees, their places of residence, and the dates of their patents, with an alphabetical list of the names of the patentees; also, all the acts passed by Congress on the subject of patents* (Washington, D.C., printed and sold by S. Alfred Elliot, July 20th, 1820).

3. William Elliot, *The Patentee's Manual; Containing a list of patents granted by the United States for the Encouragement of Arts and Sciences, alphabetically arranged, from 1790 to 1830; . . . also, the Laws of Congress for granting patents; with a digest of all the decisions which have taken place in the courts of the United States respecting patents* (Washington, printed by S. A. Elliot, 1830).

4. Leonard D. White, *The Jeffersonians: A Study in Administrative History, 1801-1829* (New York, Macmillan, 1951), pp. 183-210.

5. Patent Office, *The Story of the United States Patent Office, 1790-1956* [Washington, Government Printing Office, 1956].

6. White, p. 210.

7. Patent Office, *List of Patents Granted by the United States from April 10, 1790 to December 31, 1836* (Washington, Commissioner of Patents, 1872).

8. Department of State, Miscellaneous Letters, 1790-1820 [original manuscript letters preserved in the National Archives].

9. Wilhelmus Bogart Bryan, *A History of the National Capital* (2 vols. New York, Macmillan, 1914), *2*, 78.

10. William Dawson Johnston, *History of the Library of Congress . . .* 1800-1864 (Washington, Government Printing Office, 1904), p. 111.

11. *National Intelligencer,* Vol. *22,* No. 6589, March 24, 1834.

12. Bryan, *2,* 78.

13. Ibid., p. 27. William Elliot, *The Washington Guide . . .* (Washington, S. A. Elliot, 1822). Editions issued in 1826 and 1830, published by S. A. Elliot, and 1837, published by Franck Taylor, are in the Library of Congress.

14. Patent Office, *List of Patents . . . 1790-1836,* Appendix.

15. Bryan, *2,* 2 n.

16. Ibid., *2,* 222. It is accepted in this paper that the names S. Elliot, Seth Elliot, S. A. Elliot, Alfred Elliot, and S. Alfred Elliot, all of which appear in existing documents, are forms of name used at one time or another by Seth Alfred Elliot.

17. Patent Office, *List of Patents . . . 1790-1836.*

18. *Repertory of the Arts.* London, printed for G. and T. Wilke, 1794-1825. Vols. *1-16,* 1794-1802; 2d ser. Vols. *1-46,* 1802-1825. Monthly.

19. Department of State, Miscellaneous Letters.

20. White, p. 189.

21. Department of State, Miscellaneous Letters.

22. See notes 2 and 3 of this section.

23. Patent Office, *List of Patents . . . 1790-1836,* Appendix.

24. Johnston, p. 372.

25. *The Washington Guide* (Washington City, F. Taylor, 1837), pp. 237-38.

Jewett's "Copy-right Publications"

1. Joseph A. Borome, *Charles Coffin Jewett* (Chicago, American Library Association, 1951), p. 27.

2. Act of Aug. 10, 1846, c. 178, sec. 10, 9 STAT. 106.

3. Borome, p. 31.

4. Ibid., pp. 28-29.

5. Letter in the Archives Collection of Brown University, quoted in Borome, pp. 40-41.

6. UNESCO/Library of Congress Bibliographical Survey, "Second Interim Report of the UNESCO/Library of Congress Bibliographical Planning Group," by Kathrine Oliver Murra (Appendix to Library of Congress *Information Bulletin* Sept. 13-19, 1949), p. 33.

7. Smithsonian Institution, *Annual Report . . . 1849,* p. 36.

8. Ibid., *1850,* p. 146 ff.

9. Ibid., p. 28.

10. *Catalogue of the Library of Congress . . . December, 1839. Supplement . . . December 1, 1846,* p. 10.

11. Act of Feb. 5, 1859, c. 22, sec. 8, 11 STAT. 380.

12. Smithsonian Institution, *Annual Report . . . 1852,* pp. 39-40.

13. Ibid., *1851,* p. 23.

14. Ibid., *1852,* p. 37.

15. Ibid., *1854,* p. 21. A full review of the conflict between Jewett and Henry may be found in Borome, pp. 87-106.

16. Smithsonian Institution, *Annual Report . . . 1856,* p. 40.

17. Ibid., *1854,* pp. 23-24.

18. UNESCO/Library of Congress Bibliographical Survey. *Bibliographical Services . . .* , Appendix: Notes on the Development of the Concept of Current Complete National Bibliography, by Kathrine Oliver Murra (Washington, 1950), pp. [1], 2.

19. Act of Feb. 5, 1859, c. 22, sec. 8, 11 STAT. 380-81.

20. Library of Congress, *Report . . . 1946,* pp. 71-78.

21. Johnston, pp. 347-48, 383-84.

22. Ibid., p. 365.

23. Library of Congress, *Alphabetical Catalogue of the Library of Congress: Authors* (Washington, Government Printing Office, 1864), p. 4.

CHAPTER 3 THE ACT OF MARCH 3, 1891
Underlying Bibliographical and Trade Motivations

1. Johnston, *History of the Library of Congress,* p. 384.

2. Library of Congress, *Report . . . 1946,* pp. 113-14, 99.

3. Ibid., p. 114.

4. Act of Mar. 3, 1865, c. 126, 13 STAT. 540.

5. Library of Congress, *Report . . . 1946,* p. 99.

6. Ibid., pp. 116-17.

7. Act of July 8, 1870, c. 230, 16 STAT. 212.

8. Library of Congress, *Report . . . 1946,* pp. 99-100.

9. Ainsworth Rand Spofford, *The Copyright System of the United States—Its Origin and Its Growth,* (Washington, Press of Gedney & Roberts Co., 1892), from *Celebration of the Beginning of the Second Century of the American Patent System at Washington City, D.C., April 8, 9, 10, 1891,* pp. 149-60.

10. Arthur E. Bestor, Jr., "The Transformation of American Scholarship, 1875-1917," in Pierce Butler, ed., *Librarians, Scholars, and Booksellers at Mid-Century . . .* (Chicago, University of Chicago Press [c. 1953]), p. 12.

11. Ibid., p. 17.

12. *Library Journal, 1,* Nos. 2-3 (Nov. 30, 1876), 140-43.

13. Bestor, p. 17.

14. *Library Journal, 29,* No. 12 (Dec. 1904), 252-53.

15. Henry Stevens, "Photobibliography; A Word on Catalogues and How to Make Them," in his *Bibliotheca Geographica & Historica* (London, Henry Stevens, 1872), pp. [1]-14.

16. For example, see Henry R. Tedder, "The Official Record of Current Literature," in Bibliographical Society (London), *Transactions, 1* (1893), 147-[64]. Also *Library Association Record,* No. 11 (Nov. 15, 1909), 517.

17. This may be observed by scanning the "Bibliography of Co-operative Cataloging" by Thorstein Jahr and Adam Julius Strohm, printed as an appendix to the annual report of the Librarian of Congress for 1902, pp. 109-205.

18. Herbert Putnam, "Bibliographic Bureaus," *Library Journal, 12,* Nos. 9-10 (Sept.-Oct., 1887), 409-13, 450-52.

19. John Russell Bartlett, *Bibliotheca Americana: a Catalogue of Books Relating to North and South America in the library of John Carter Brown* . . . (4 vols. Providence, 1865-71).

20. *American Catalogue* . . . *1876-1884* (New York, Office of the Publishers' Weekly, 1885), p. viii.

21. Joseph N. Whitten and Aaron L. Fessler, "Hard-cover Reprint Publishing," *Library Trends,* 7, No. 1 (July 1958), 84.

22. Ibid.

23. Lehmann-Haupt, *The Book in America,* p. 210.

Factors Influencing the Form and Content of the Cataloging Provisions

1. Act of July 8, 1870, c. 230, sec. 85, 16 STAT. 212.

2. H.R. 1714, 41st Cong., 2d Sess. (1870).

3. *Congressional Globe,* 41st Cong., 2d Sess., p. 2684.

4. Library of Congress, *Report* . . . *1871,* p. 6.

5. Ibid., *1872,* p. 5.

6. Act of June 18, 1874, c. 301, 18 STAT. 78.

7. Ainsworth Rand Spofford, "Copyright in Its Relation to Libraries and Literature," *Library Journal, 1,* Nos. 2-3 (Nov. 30, 1876), 89.

8. Library of Congress, *Report* . . . *1872,* p. 7.

9. Ibid., *1874,* p. 7.

10. Ibid., *1885,* p. 7.

11. Copyright Office, *Copyright in Congress, 1789-1904* (Washington, Government Printing Office, 1905), p. 51.

12. U. S. Congress, Senate Committee on Patents, *International Copyright. Statements* . . . *Relating to the Bill* (*S. 1178*), p. 72.

13. Ibid., p. 104. See also p. 77.

14. Ibid., p. 72.

15. Ibid., p. 105.

16. George Haven Putnam, *The Question of Copyright* (New York, G. P. Putnam's Sons, 1891), p. 386.

17. Ibid., p. 53.

18. *Congressional Record, 22* (Pt. 1), 7, 32-38, 55-60. [Dec. 1-3, 1890.]

19. Ibid., *22* (Pt. 3), 2381. [Feb. 9, 1891.]

20. Ibid., p. 2392. [Feb. 9, 1891.]

21. Ibid., p. 2602. [Feb. 13, 1891.]

22. Ibid., pp. 2617-18. [Feb. 13, 1891.]

23. Ibid., *22* (Pt. 4), 3882-88.

24. Putnam, p. x.

25. Copyright Office, Stenographic Report of the Proceedings . . . of the Conference on Copyright (3 vols. 1905-06), *2*, 174-76.

26. Act of Mar. 3, 1891, c. 565, sec. 4, 26 STAT. 1108.

CHAPTER 4 THE CATALOG OF COPYRIGHT ENTRIES, 1891-1909

Description

1. Treasury Department, *Catalogue of Title-Entries of Books and Other Articles entered in the office of the Librarian of Congress, at Washington, under the copyright law, from July 1 to July 11, 1891, inclusive, wherein the copyright has been completed by the deposit of two copies in the office* (Washington, Government Printing Office, 1891). For the most part, title changes are disregarded in the text; the full title is normally shortened simply to "the *Catalog*."

2. Library of Congress, *Report* . . . *1892*, pp. 4-5.

3. Ibid., *1897*, p. 14.

4. Ibid., *1900*, p. 39.

5. Ibid., *1901*, p. 56.

Factors Influencing Development

1. *Library Journal, 16*, No. 12 (Dec. 1891), 117.

2. *American Catalogue, 1884-1890*, p. vii.

3. Tedder, Bibliographical Society (London), *Transactions, 1* (1893), 147-64.

4. Ibid., p. 150.

5. Stevens, "Photobibliography," in *Bibliotheca Geographica & Historica.*

6. Tedder, p. 156.

7. George Watson Cole, "American Bibliography, General and Local," *Library Journal, 19,* No. 1 (Jan. 1894), 5.

8. Ibid., p. 7.

9. Samuel H. Ranck, "Need of Additional Copyright Depositories," *Library Journal, 20,* No. 12 (Dec. 1895), 43-45.

10. *Library Journal, 20,* No. 12 (Dec. 1895), 78.

11. *American Catalogue, 1890-95,* p. viii.

12. U. S. Congress, Joint Committee on the Library, *Condition of the Library of Congress* (March 3, 1897), p. 226.

13. J. C. M. Hanson, "Thorvald Solberg, the First Register of Copyrights," *Scandinavia, 1,* No. 2 (Feb. 1924), [75].

14. Thorvald Solberg, "Thorvald Solberg. An Autobiographical Sketch," *Town and Country Review,* Sept. 1937. Reprinted in Thorvald Solberg, *Copyright Miscellany* (Boston, Luce, 1939), Item One.

15. *Publishers' Weekly,* No. 133 (Aug. 1, 1874), p. 141.

16. Hanson, p. 76.

17. Richard Rogers Bowker, *Copyright, Its Law and Its Literature . . . with a Bibliography of Literary Property by Thorvald Solberg* (New York, Publishers' Weekly, 1886).

18. Solberg, ". . . Autobiographical Sketch."

19. Thorvald Solberg, Letters to J. C. M. Hanson, Nov. 17 and 24, 1923, in Copyright Office, Special Memoranda Letter Book, 1903-1923 [i.e. 1924].

20. *Bulletin of Bibliography, 1,* No. 3 (Oct. 1897), [35].

21. New York Library Club, [Proceedings, meeting of March 11, 1897,] *Library Journal, 22,* No. 4 (April 1897), 210.

22. U. S. Congress, Joint Committee on the Library, *Condition of the Library of Congress,* p. 228.

23. Richard Rogers Bowker, "Bibliographical Endeavors in America," *Library Journal, 22,* No. 8 (Aug. 1897), 387.

24. UNESCO/Library of Congress Bibliographical Survey. *Bibliographical Services . . . ,* Appendix, pp. 10-11.

25. J. C. M. Hanson, "The Library of Congress and Its New Catalogue, in *Essays Offered to Herbert Putnam,* p. 184. Quotation by permission of the Yale University Press.

26. Library of Congress, *Report . . . 1897,* p. 14.

27. Ibid., *1898,* p. 13.

28. Ibid., p. 22.

29. Ibid., p. 21.

30. *Library Journal, 23,* No. 8 (Aug. 1898), 118.

31. Ibid., pp. 118-19.

32. William Stetson Merrill, "General and National Bibliographies," in Bibliographical Society of Chicago, *Year-book, 1899-1900,* pp. 21, 24-25.

33. Bibliographical Society of Chicago, *Year-book, 1900-1901,* pp. 18-19.

34. Aksel G. S. Josephson, "Plan for the Organization of an Institute for Bibliographical Research," in Bibliographical Society of Chicago, *Year-book, 1901-1902,* pp. 57-59.

35. Ainsworth Rand Spofford, *A Book for All Readers* (New York, G. P. Putnam's Sons, 1900), p. 465.

36. Ibid., pp. 474-75.

37. *American Catalogue, 1895-1900,* p. [iii].

38. Library of Congress, *Report . . . 1899,* p. 3.

39. Ibid., *1902,* p. 79.

40. Charles Harris Hastings, "Reminiscences and Observations on the Card Distribution Work of the Library of Congress," in *Essays Offered to Herbert Putnam,* p. [195].

41. Ibid., pp. 198-99.

42. Frederick W. Ashley, "Relations of the Copyright Office to the Library of Congress." [Memorandum to the Register of Copyrights, Dec. 1, 1908.]

43. "The National Library: Its Work and Functions," *Library Journal, 26,* No. 12 (Dec. 1901), 855-58.

44. *Library Journal, 27,* No. 6 (June 1902), 318-19.

45. Alice Bertha Kroeger, *Guide to the Study and Use of Reference Books,* issued by the Publishing Board of the American Library Association (Boston, Houghton Mifflin, 1902), p. 69.

46. Library of Congress, *Report . . . 1902,* pp. 59-60.

47. Roberts, *Records in the Copyright Office . . . 1790-1870,* p. 15. Frederick R. Goff, *The First Decade of the Federal Act for Copyright, 1790-1800* (Washington, Library of Congress, c. 1951), p. 8.

48. Library of Congress, *Report . . . 1903,* p. 93.

49. Ibid., *1902,* p. 90.

50. John Lawrence Lawlor, *The H. W. Wilson Company: Half a Century of Bibliographic Publishing* (Minneapolis, University of Minnesota Press, [c. 1950]), p. 25.

51. Ibid., p. 28.

52. Van Hoesen, *Bibliography*, p. 221.

53. Lawlor, p. 32.

54. H. W. Wilson Company, *A Quarter Century of Cumulative Bibliography* (New York, H. W. Wilson Company, 1923), p. 11.

55. Lawlor, p. 138.

56. Ibid., pp. 59-60.

57. Herbert Putnam, "The Library of Congress as a National Library," *Library Journal, 30*, No. 9 (Sept. 1905), 29.

58. Ibid., p. 32.

59. U.S. Congress, House of Representatives, 58th Cong., 2d Sess., *Printing of Treasury Department Publications and Catalogue of Title Entries*, Document No. 420, p. 3.

60. Ibid., p. 7.

61. Ibid., p. 8.

62. Library of Congress, *Report . . . 1906*, p. 93.

63. Ibid., *1907*, p. 107.

64. Bibliographical Society of America, *Proceedings and Papers, 1*, Pt. 2 (1906-07), 117.

65. Thorvald Solberg, Letter to James Bain, July 7, 1906, in Copyright Office, Catalogue of Copyright Entries Letter Book, July 1906-October 1916.

66. *American Catalog, 1905-07*, p. vi.

CHAPTER 5 THE ACT OF MARCH 4, 1909

The Cataloging Provisions of the Memorandum Draft Bill of October 23, 1905

1. Copyright Office, Special Memoranda Letter Book, 1905-1923 [i.e. 1924]. Memorandum, June 5, 1905.

2. Copyright Office, Stenographic Report, 2, 5. The Memorandum Draft Bill is reproduced in full in Vol. 2.

3. U.S. Congress, House of Representatives, 58th Cong., 2d Sess., Document No. 420.

Discussion of the Cataloging Provisions

1. Copyright Office, Stenographic Report, 2, 201 ff.

2. Ibid., pp. 137-88.

3. *Library Journal, 32,* No. 1 (Jan. 1907), 14-16. Progress of the Copyright Bill was reported at some length in library periodicals in 1906, 1907, and 1908.

4. Copyright Office, Stenographic Report, *2,* 193-94.

5. Ibid., pp. 195-96.

6. Ibid., p. 196.

7. Ibid., pp. 197-98.

8. Ibid., pp. 200-1.

9. Ibid., p. 201.

10. Ibid., pp. 202-3.

11. Ibid., p. 205.

12. Ibid., pp. 122-23.

13. Ibid., p. 204.

14. Ibid., pp. 204, 206.

15. Ibid., p. 209.

16. Ibid., pp. 218, 219.

17. Ibid., p. 418.

18. Ibid., pp. 421-22.

19. Ibid., p. 425.

20. Ibid., p. 9.

21. U.S. Congress, Committees on Patents, *Arguments . . . on the bills S. 6330 and H.R. 19853.* Dec. 7, 8, 10, and 11, 1906 (Washington, Government Printing Office, 1906), pp. 121-26.

22. Ibid., p. 399.

The Cataloging Provisions as Adopted

1. Judith Caro, "Legislative history of copyright searches." [Memorandum to the Register of Copyrights, Feb. 6, 1953.]

CHAPTER 6 OPERATIONS UNDER THE CATALOGING PROVISIONS OF THE ACT OF 1909 THROUGH WORLD WAR II

1. Library of Congress, *Report . . . 1910,* p. 98.

2. UNESCO/Library of Congress Bibliographical Survey, *Bibliographical Services,* p. 11.

3. Charles Harris Hastings, "Delay in supplying cards for new copyright books." Thorvald Solberg, "The forwarding of copyright books

for cataloging." [Memoranda to the Librarian of Congress, Oct. 22 and 27, 1909, respectively.]

4. Library of Congress, *Report . . . 1910*, p. 98.

5. Ibid., *1911*, pp. 106-7.

6. Copyright Office, Special Memoranda Letter Book, memorandum, April 22, 1920.

7. Ibid., letter to Ligon Johnson, July 17, 1923.

8. Ibid., letter to R. R. Bowker, July 21, 1923.

9. Library of Congress, *Report . . . 1925*, pp. 187-88.

10. Copyright Office, Special Memoranda Letter Book, letter to J. C. M. Hanson, Nov. 17, 1923.

11. Ibid., letter to R. R. Bowker, June 9, 1923.

12. Ibid., letter to R. R. Bowker, Aug. 28, 1923.

13. H.R. 9137, 68th Cong., 1st Sess. (1924).

14. H.R. 12425, 72d Cong., 1st Sess. (1932).

15. S. 3047, 74th Cong., 1st Sess. (1935).

16. S. 3043, 76th Cong., 3d Sess. (1940).

17. H.R. 12549, 71st Cong., 3d Sess. (1931).

18. H.R. 11258, 68th Cong., 2d Sess. (1925).

19. Abe A. Goldman, "The History of U.S.A. Copyright Law Revision from 1901 to 1954," Study No. 1 in *Copyright Law Revision: Studies . . . pursuant to S. Res. 53, Studies 1-4* (issued as a committee print by the Senate Committee on the Judiciary, Washington, Government Printing Office, 1960). See especially pp. 4-11.

20. Solberg, ". . . Autobiographical Sketch."

Index

Compiled by Kathleen Leerburger